Systematic Theology for Teens - Build Your Statement of Faith

Teen-Friendly Christian Doctrine - Bible Verses for Hard Questions, and a Guided Walk with Jesus to Build a Faith You Can Defend

Matthew R. Caldwell

Contents

SYSTEMATIC THEOLOGY FOR TEENS

Build Your Statement of Faith

MATTHEW R. CALDWELL

Foundation: You're Allowed to Ask

Cold Open Moment

You know the feeling.

You're sitting in a youth group circle, or maybe riding in the passenger seat of your parent's car, and someone says something about God. They say it with absolute confidence. Everyone else nods.

But inside your head, a massive error code just flashed. *Wait, if God is perfectly good, why did He let that happen?* or *If grace is free, why do I feel like I constantly have to earn my spot?*

In that split second, you have a choice. You can raise your hand, stop the conversation, and ask the question that's burning a hole in your brain. You can risk looking like the one person in the room who doesn't "get it."

Or, you can do what most of us have done a hundred times: you smile, nod, and swallow the question.

You stay quiet because you've quietly bought into a terrifying lie: that asking a hard theological question means you are losing your faith. You worry that if you pull on that loose thread, the whole sweater is going to unravel. So you just keep scrolling, keep smiling, and keep pretending it all makes perfect sense.

But swallowed questions don't disappear. They just turn into quiet doubts.

Big Idea

God isn't intimidated by your questions, and your faith shouldn't be either.

Why This Matters

You might be thinking, "Can't I just love Jesus and not worry about deep theology? Isn't this stuff just for pastors and guys with elbow patches on their jackets?"

No. Because whether you realize it or not, you are already a theologian. Everyone is.

When your friend texts you about a massive panic attack and asks where God is, your response is theology. When you scroll through TikTok and see a viral video tearing apart a Bible verse, how you process that is theology. When you mess up on a Friday night and wake up on Saturday wondering if God is officially done with you, your answer to that fear is theology.

- If you don't know what you believe, you will just absorb whatever the internet hands you.
- If you just borrow your parents' or your pastor's answers, your faith will crack the second you leave home.

You need a faith that belongs to you. You need a faith that can survive a group chat debate, a brutal season of suffering, and your own late-night overthinking. And building that kind of faith always starts with giving yourself permission to ask real questions.

Key Words

- **Theology:** The study of discovering who God is and how He works in the world.
- **Doctrine:** A specific teaching or belief about God that is drawn from the Bible (like the doctrine of the Trinity, or the doctrine of sin).
- **Doubt:** The feeling of being uncertain about what is true, which is a normal human experience rather than a sin.
- **Faith:** Trusting God based on what He has revealed, even when you don't have all the answers.

Precision Note (grown-up wording): Theology is the application of Scripture by persons to every area of life.

Bible Receipts

You aren't expected to turn your brain off to follow Jesus. In fact, Christians believe God gave you a mind on purpose.

Let's look at how the Bible actually handles people with questions.

First, look at a guy who brought his raw, unfiltered doubt straight to Jesus. In Mark 9, a father brings his deeply suffering son to Jesus for healing.

The father is desperate, but his faith is hanging by a thread. He says to Jesus, "If you can do anything, have compassion on us and help us."

Jesus challenges the "if you can" part. And the father immediately cries out, "I do believe; help my unbelief!" (Mark 9:24, CSB).

Jesus didn't walk away from him. He didn't shame him for his imperfect theology or his hesitation. He healed the boy. Jesus meets us exactly where our fragile faith collides with our honest questions.

Second, the Bible actually praises people who double-check the facts. In the book of Acts, the Apostle Paul goes to a town called Berea to preach. He's the most famous Christian leader in the world at this point. But the people there didn't just blindly swallow what he said.

Acts 17:11 (CSB) says, "The people here were of more noble character... since they received the word with eagerness and examined the Scriptures daily to see if these things were so." God calls it "noble" to open your Bible and verify the truth.

Finally, read the Psalms. The book of Psalms is the playlist of the Bible, and it is packed with agonizing questions. David routinely yells at God. "How long, LORD? Will you forget me forever? How long will you hide your face from me?" (Psalm 13:1, CSB).

If God hated our questions, He wouldn't have put an entire book of them right in the middle of our Bibles.

Truth in Plain English

Let's get something straight right at the beginning of this book.

You are not dumb for wanting things to make sense. You aren't a "bad Christian" because certain Bible verses confuse you, or because you find it hard to understand how a loving God allows cancer, depression, or heartbreak.

Highlightable line: God would rather have your honest questions than your fake confidence.

For a long time, church culture has sometimes made teens feel like the goal is simply to "just believe." But blind faith is actually quite dangerous. If you don't know *why* you believe what you believe, anyone with a microphone and a charismatic personality can talk you out of it.

We aren't going to do that in this book. We aren't going to dodge the hard stuff.

We are going to look at the massive, beautiful, sometimes heavy truths of the Christian faith. We're going to look at the Bible. And we're going to build your theology brick by brick.

Common Confusion Box

Confusion #1: "Good Christians don't have doubts." This sounds right because the loudest people in church often seem 100% certain about absolutely everything. It feels like everyone else has a VIP pass to absolute clarity, while you're stuck in the nosebleed section of confusion. But it's wrong. It leads to a culture of hiding. If you read the Bible, you'll see that the greatest heroes of the faith, Abraham, Moses, Elijah, Peter, all had moments of profound doubt and hesitation.

Doubt isn't the opposite of faith. Refusing to trust God is the opposite of faith. Doubt is just a pothole on the road of trust; it doesn't mean you've driven off a cliff.

Confusion #2: "If I start asking questions, I'll lose my faith." This sounds right because we've all seen videos of people "deconstructing" their faith online, and it usually starts with a question. But here is what Scripture shows instead: truth has nothing to fear from investigation. If Christianity is actually true, it can handle your hardest questions. It can handle your deepest scrutiny. God is not fragile.

Highlightable line: A faith that can't be questioned is a faith that can't be trusted.

Why This Changes Real Life

This book is going to challenge you to do something hard but entirely worth it.

Over the next several chapters, you aren't just going to read about theology. You are going to write it. By the end of this journey, you are going to have a 1-Page Personal Statement of Faith.

You're going to know exactly what you believe about God, Jesus, the Holy Spirit, sin, the church, and your own purpose. You're going to know the Bible verses that back those beliefs up. You are going to have a 30-Second script you can actually speak out loud when someone asks you what you believe.

And most importantly, you are going to create a "When I Doubt" plan, a concrete strategy for what to do when your emotions are spiraling and your faith feels weak.

This changes real life because it moves you out of the passenger seat. You won't just be riding on the momentum of your youth pastor's energy or your parents' habits.

When the group chat turns toxic, you'll have a theological anchor for how to treat people. When your anxiety spikes at 2:00 AM, you'll have a deeply rooted doctrine of God's sovereignty to fall back on. When you fail and feel crushed by guilt, you won't have to guess if God still loves you, you'll have your doctrine of salvation written down in your own words.

Highlightable line: Borrowed faith collapses under pressure, but built faith stands firm.

How to Use This Book

1. **Be brutally honest.** If a chapter doesn't make sense, circle it. If you disagree, write your frustration in the margins. This is your book.
2. **Read the receipts.** Don't just take my word for it. Open your Bible and read the CSB references provided.
3. **Build your bricks.** At the end of every chapter, there is a "Belief Builder" section. Do not skip this. This is the engine of the whole project. Each one is a brick that you will eventually use to build your final Statement of Faith.
4. **Read it your way.** You can read this book solo, discuss it with a parent, or use it as a youth group study.

Are you ready? It's time to start building.

Try This This Week

Get a physical sticky note or a small piece of paper. Write down the absolute biggest, most intimidating question you currently have about God, the Bible, or Christianity.

Don't try to answer it. Don't try to make it sound pretty or "churchy." Just write the raw question. Fold it in half and stick it inside the front cover of your Bible. You are giving yourself permission to carry that question with you as we begin.

Talk It Out

- When was the last time you had a question about God but kept it to yourself? Why did you stay quiet?
- Why do you think it feels risky or dangerous to ask deep theological questions in church?
- How are you planning to use this book? (Are you reading solo, with a friend, with a mentor, or in a youth group?)
- What is one topic in Christianity that currently feels confusing or frustrating to you?

BELIEF BUILDER (Brick #0: Foundation)

My one-sentence belief: "I believe it is safe to bring my real, honest questions to a real God."

Bible receipts (pick 1–2): Mark 9:24; Acts 17:11; Psalm 13:1

This changes my life because: "I don't have to fake being a perfect Christian; I can grow by seeking the truth without fear."

One question I still have: (Write one honest question. No pretending.)

Short Prayer

Father, thank You that You are not intimidated by my confusion. Jesus, thank You for meeting me in my doubts just like You met others. Holy Spirit, give me the courage to ask hard questions as I read this book. Keep me from faking it. Guide my mind to understand the truth, and anchor my heart in Your love. Amen.

Brick-by-Brick: How to Build Your Personal Statement of Faith

Cold Open Moment

You're sitting across from a friend at lunch, and the conversation takes a weird, sudden turn. They know you go to church, so they ask a direct question: "So, what do you actually believe about all that?"

Your brain completely freezes.

You scramble to find words that don't sound like a copy-pasted youth group answer. You eventually mumble something like, 'Well, I just believe God loves me, and Jesus died for my sins.'

It's completely true. But as you say it out loud, it feels flimsy. It feels like you're giving a summary of a movie you haven't actually watched. And as your friend nods and changes the subject, a quiet panic sets in: *What if they had asked a follow-up question? What if they asked why?*

You realize in that moment that you have a lot of feelings about God, but you don't actually have the words to explain Him. You have pieces of a puzzle, but no picture on the box to show you how they fit together.

Big Idea

Your faith shouldn't be a random pile of borrowed opinions; it should be a solid house you know how to build and defend.

Why This Matters

For the rest of this book, you are going to be building a Personal Statement of Faith.

Usually, a "statement of faith" is a dry, boring page on a church's website that nobody reads. It outlines their official positions on everything from the Bible to the end of the world. But a *personal* statement is different. It is your stake in the ground.

If you don't define what you believe, the culture around you will gladly define it for you. You need to write this down because:

- **It acts as an anchor.** When your emotions are lying to you, your written statement reminds you of what is objectively true.
- **It kills the panic.** When someone challenges your faith, you won't have to scramble for words because you've already done the hard work of thinking it through.

By the end of this book, you won't just have a head full of facts. You will have a 1-page document, written by you, that declares exactly who God is and where you stand.

Key Words

- **Statement of Faith:** A written summary of the core truths you believe about God, the Bible, and the world.
- **Core Doctrine:** The non-negotiable truths of Christianity that hold the whole religion together (like the resurrection of Jesus).
- **Secondary Issues:** Important beliefs where faithful Christians disagree (like how to baptize people), but that don't determine your salvation.
- **Conviction:** A strong belief you live by, based on seeing it clearly in the Bible, even if other faithful Christians might see it differently.

Precision Note (grown-up wording): Theological triage is the process of ranking doctrines by their importance to the gospel, separating absolute essentials from secondary disagreements.

Bible Receipts

You might wonder if writing a statement of faith is actually biblical. It absolutely is. The early Christians were constantly summarizing their core beliefs so they wouldn't get distracted by whatever new theory was trending.

Look at the Apostle Paul in 1 Corinthians. The church in Corinth was a mess, arguing about everything under the sun. Paul writes to them to pull them back to the center.

He says, "For I passed on to you as most important what I also received: that Christ died for our sins according to the Scriptures, that he was buried, that he was raised on the third day..." (1 Corinthians 15:3-4, CSB). Notice his phrasing: *as most important*. Paul had a ranking system. He knew what the absolute core of the faith was, and he made sure the church knew it too.

Then, look at how we are supposed to talk about these beliefs. In Ephesians 4:14-15 (CSB), Paul tells believers they need to grow up so they won't be "tossed by the waves and blown around by every wind of teaching."

How do we stop getting blown around? By "speaking the truth in love." The goal isn't just to be correct. The goal is to hold onto the truth with a massive amount of love for the people around you.

Truth in Plain English

To build your Statement of Faith, we are going to use the Belief Builder system. At the end of every chapter, you will write one "brick." By the time you reach the end of the book, you will assemble all those bricks into your final document.

But as we build, you need to know that not every theological brick is the same size. Some things are massive, load-bearing walls. Other things are just the paint color in the living room.

Think of theology like a target with three circles.

The bullseye is **Core Doctrine**. This is the heartbeat. God is a Trinity. Jesus is fully God and fully man. Jesus physically rose from the dead. Salvation is by grace alone. If you remove the bullseye, the whole faith collapses. We defend the core fiercely.

The next ring out is **Convictions**. These are important issues that shape how you worship or do church, but they don't decide if you go to heaven. This includes things like how a church is governed, or whether babies should be baptized or just adults. You should have strong convictions, but you must recognize that faithful, Bible-loving Christians disagree on these things.

The outer ring is **Opinions**. These are things the Bible isn't totally clear on. What kind of music should we play on Sunday? What is the exact timeline of the end of the world?

Highlightable line: You don't have to win every argument to be faithful, but you do have to know what's worth fighting for.

Common Confusion Box

Confusion #1: "If Christians disagree on something, it means the Bible is broken." This sounds right because when Christians argue online, it looks chaotic and messy. It makes it seem like nobody actually knows what the truth is. But it's wrong. The Bible is perfect, but our human brains are limited. God gave us absolute clarity on the core (how to be saved), and He allows us to wrestle through the secondary issues so we can learn humility.

Highlightable line: Disagreement isn't proof that God is silent; it's proof that humans are still learning.

Confusion #2: "If I'm right about the Bible, I'm allowed to be aggressive about it." This sounds right because our culture rewards people who loudly "destroy" their opponents in debates. But here is what Scripture shows instead: truth without love is just noise. James 1:20 (CSB) clearly says, "Human anger does not accomplish God's righteousness." You can have perfectly correct theology, but if you treat people like garbage while defending it, you are misrepresenting Jesus.

Highlightable line: True theological confidence makes you kind, not arrogant.

Why This Changes Real Life

Knowing the difference between core doctrines and secondary opinions is a total game-changer for your daily life.

You are growing up in a world that is obsessed with fighting. Social media is a constant warzone of people screaming at each other over every tiny issue. And unfortunately, sometimes church group chats or youth group circles look exactly the same.

When you build your Statement of Faith, you learn how to disagree well.

If someone attacks a core doctrine, like saying Jesus was just a good teacher, not God, you will know exactly how to stand your ground and defend the truth clearly. You won't panic, because you know your foundation.

But if a friend at a different church believes a different theory about how the end times will happen, you won't ruin a friendship over it. You will be able to smile, discuss it calmly, and say, "I see it differently, but we both love Jesus, so we're family."

You get to be the calmest person in the room. When you actually know what you believe, you don't have to raise your voice to prove it.

Try This This Week

Get the physical space ready for your Statement of Faith project.

Find a blank notebook, a clean document on your laptop, or create a new dedicated note in your phone. Title it: *My Personal Statement of Faith*. You don't have to write any deep theology in it today. Just set the space aside. You are making a physical commitment to finish what we are starting.

Talk It Out

- When was a time you felt pressured to explain your faith to someone, but felt totally unprepared?
- Why is it so much easier for Christians to fight about outer-circle "opinions" than to talk about inner-circle "core doctrines"?
- What do you think is the difference between being confident in what you believe, and being arrogant about it?
- Look at the three circles (Core, Conviction, Opinion). What is one belief you think belongs in the center bullseye?

BELIEF BUILDER (Brick #0.2: The Goal)

My one-sentence belief: "I believe knowing what is true about God is worth the effort, and I want a faith that is deeply my own."

Bible receipts (pick 1–2): 1 Corinthians 15:3–4; Ephesians 4:14–15

This changes my life because: "I can stop panicking when someone challenges my faith, because I am learning exactly what I believe and why."

One question I still have: (Write one honest question. No pretending.)

Short Prayer

Father, I want a faith that is real and resilient. Jesus, thank You for being the absolute center of everything I believe. Holy Spirit, give me the endurance to finish this project. When I am confused, give me clarity. When I think I know everything, give me humility. Amen.

PART 1 - THE BIBLE: How We Know What’s True

In this part, we’re laying the foundation for everything else: **how we know what’s true and why the Bible deserves your trust.** We’ll talk about what the Bible is, why Christians treat it as God’s Word, and how to read it without twisting it, or getting lost. The goal isn’t to win arguments online. The goal is confidence. By the end of this part, you’ll be able to write the first section of your Personal Statement of Faith: **what you believe about the Bible, why you believe it, and how you’ll use it when questions hit.**

Brick #1: Why Trust the Bible?

Cold Open Moment

You've probably seen the viral videos. A guy with a microphone stands on a college campus or a city sidewalk, interviewing Christians.

He shoves the mic in someone's face and asks, "Why do you believe Christianity is true?" The Christian usually answers, "Because the Bible says so." Then comes the trap. The interviewer smirks and asks, "Okay, but why do you trust the Bible? Isn't it just a really old book written by primitive guys in the desert? Hasn't it been translated like a giant game of telephone?"

Suddenly, the Christian freezes. They don't know what to say.

And if you're honest, watching a video like that might make your stomach drop, too. Because maybe you've wondered the exact same thing.

You hold this book in your hands at church, but in the back of your mind, a quiet voice whispers: *What if it really is just a human book? What if we are just guessing about who God is?*

If you can't trust the Bible, your entire faith is just a fragile house of cards waiting for the wind to blow. You need to know if this book can actually hold the weight of your life.

Big Idea

The Bible isn't just a book of human advice about God; it is God's actual words given to humans, which means we can trust it completely.

Why This Matters

This is the foundation for everything else you will ever believe. Every other brick in your Statement of Faith rests entirely on this one.

If the Bible is just a human book, a collection of ancient diaries and good advice, then it has no real authority over your life. You can just pick the parts you like and throw away the parts that challenge you. But if it is actually God speaking, everything changes.

- **It gives you an anchor.** When culture constantly shifts its definition of truth, the Bible gives you ground that doesn't move.
- **It reveals the invisible.** You don't have to guess what God thinks about you, your sin, or your future, because He already wrote it down.

Key Words

- **Revelation:** God choosing to reveal Himself to us, because we could never figure Him out on our own.
- **Inspiration:** The Holy Spirit guiding the human authors of the Bible so that what they wrote is exactly what God wanted to say.
- **Authority:** Because the Bible is God's word, it has the final say over what is true and how we should live.
- **Inerrancy:** The belief that the original manuscripts of the Bible are completely true and without error.

Precision Note (grown-up wording): Christians believe in *verbal plenary inspiration*, meaning the very words themselves (verbal) and all parts of the Bible equally (plenary) are inspired by God.

Bible Receipts

The Bible doesn't actually talk about itself as a normal book. It claims something radically different.

The Apostle Paul wrote a letter to a young leader named Timothy, who was facing a culture that was violently anti-Christian. Paul didn't tell him to rely on his feelings.

He pointed him to the Book. "All Scripture is inspired by God and is profitable for teaching, for rebuking, for correcting, for training in righteousness, so that the man of God may be complete, equipped for every good work" (2 Timothy 3:16-17, CSB).

The phrase "inspired by God" literally translates to *God-breathed*. The words didn't just originate in Paul's brain; they were exhaled by the Creator.

The Apostle Peter explains how this process actually worked. He writes, "Above all, you know this: No prophecy of Scripture comes from the prophet's own interpretation, because no prophecy ever came by the will of man; instead, men spoke from God as they were carried along by the Holy Spirit" (2 Peter 1:20-21, CSB).

Notice the partnership there. Men spoke and wrote. But they were "carried along" by the Holy Spirit. God didn't erase their personalities, but He superintended the process so perfectly that the final product was entirely His truth.

Truth in Plain English

Here is how you need to think about the Bible.

It was written by over 40 different authors, over a span of 1,500 years, on three different continents, in three different languages. It includes poetry, history, letters, and prophecy. Yet, it tells one perfectly unified story from beginning to end.

God didn't just dictate the Bible like a boss talking to a robot secretary. He used King David's poetic heart. He used Paul's brilliant, logical mind.

He used Peter's raw passion. God used their vocabularies and their history. But the Holy Spirit guarded their writing so completely that the result is flawless.

Highlightable line: The Bible isn't man's best attempt to reach up to God; it's God's perfect decision to reach down to man.

When you read Scripture, you aren't just reading dead history. The Holy Spirit uses those exact words to actively speak to you today. That's why you can read a verse you've seen a hundred times, and suddenly it hits you like a freight train.

Common Confusion Box

Confusion #1: "The Bible is just a giant game of telephone." This sounds right because we know how easy it is for human stories to get twisted over time. People assume that translating the Bible from Hebrew to Greek to Latin to English corrupted it. But it's wrong. We don't have a game of telephone; we have thousands of ancient manuscripts. When scholars compare the earliest copies we have (some dating back to just decades after the New Testament was written), they match up with stunning, undeniable accuracy. The Bible is the most well-documented ancient text in human history by a massive landslide.

Highlightable line: You don't have to turn off your brain to trust your Bible; the historical evidence is on your side.

Confusion #2: "The Bible is full of contradictions." This sounds right because there are parts of the Bible that are really hard to understand, and skeptics love to copy-paste lists of "errors" from the internet. But here is what Scripture shows instead: almost every supposed "contradiction" disappears the second you read it in context. Different gospel writers didn't contradict each other; they just highlighted different details of the exact same event, like different camera angles at a sports game.

Why This Changes Real Life

Trusting the Bible is what keeps you from drowning when life gets incredibly dark.

Imagine you are going through a season where everything feels heavy. Maybe your friend group betrayed you, or your parents are fighting, or your anxiety is completely suffocating you. In that moment, your emotions will lie to you. Your brain will tell you that you are worthless, that God is angry with you, or that you are entirely alone.

If the Bible isn't true, you have no way to fight back against those lies. You just have to hope your feelings eventually change.

But if the Bible is the unbreakable word of God, you have a weapon. When your brain tells you that you are alone, you can say, "No, Psalm 34 says the Lord is near the brokenhearted. My feelings are real, but they aren't the boss. God's word is the boss."

Highlightable line: The Bible is the only voice in the universe that will never lie to you, never leave you, and never let you down.

Try This This Week

Do a "Receipt Check." The next time your pastor or youth leader teaches a lesson, open your own Bible (or Bible app) and verify that what they are saying is actually what the text says.

Don't be disrespectful, just be a Berean. Train yourself to look at the words on the page, not just the person on the stage.

Talk It Out

- When was a time you felt really confused or doubtful about something you read in the Bible?
- Why do you think it makes people so angry when Christians claim the Bible is the ultimate authority?
- If God physically spoke to you from the clouds right now, how would you listen? How should that change the way we read the Bible?
- What is the difference between respecting the Bible as a "good book" and submitting to it as "God's word"?

BELIEF BUILDER (Brick #1: About the Bible)

My one-sentence belief: "I believe the Bible is the inspired word of God, completely true and totally trustworthy."

Bible receipts (pick 1–2): 2 Timothy 3:16–17; 2 Peter 1:20–21

This changes my life because: "When my emotions and the culture lie to me, I have a solid foundation of truth to stand on."

One question I still have: (Write one honest question. No pretending.)

Short Prayer

Father, thank You for not leaving me in the dark to guess who You are. Jesus, You trusted the Scriptures completely, and I want to do the same. Holy Spirit, give me a deep hunger to read Your word. When I read things I don't understand, give me patience. When I read things I don't like, give me the humility to submit. Amen.

My Notes & Thoughts

Brick #2: How to Read the Bible Without Twisting It

Cold Open Moment

You scroll past it on Instagram every single day.

It's a beautiful picture of a sunset or a cup of coffee, and floating right in the middle is a Bible verse in a trendy font: *"I can do all things through Christ who strengthens me"* (Philippians 4:13).

Usually, the caption is about crushing a workout, passing a brutal math test, or winning a championship game. It sounds amazing. It makes Jesus feel like a cosmic energy drink sent to help you achieve your dreams.

There's just one massive problem. The guy who wrote that verse, the Apostle Paul, wasn't crushing a workout. He was locked in a filthy Roman prison, facing the possibility of execution, writing about how to survive starvation and poverty.

Suddenly, the verse isn't a hype slogan anymore. It's a survival guide for suffering.

When we rip a Bible verse out of its setting and slap it onto our own agenda, we might feel inspired, but we are actually making the Bible say something God never intended. And that is a dangerous game to play.

Big Idea

A Bible verse cannot mean what it never meant; we have to read it in context to hear what God is actually saying.

Why This Matters

Reading the Bible wrong isn't just an innocent mistake. It leads to terrible theology, and terrible theology leads to people getting hurt.

If you don't know how to read the Bible in context, you are highly vulnerable.

- **You will be easily manipulated.** Toxic leaders and internet gurus don't use a different book; they use the Bible, but they twist verses out of context to control people.
- **You will end up disappointed with God.** If you claim a verse as a "promise" that God never actually promised to you (like assuming God guarantees you will always be rich and healthy), your faith will shatter when life gets hard.

Key Words

- **Context:** The verses immediately before and after a passage, as well as the historical setting, the author, and the original audience.
- **Exegesis:** Pulling the meaning *out* of the text (this is the good way to read).
- **Eisegesis:** Shoving your own ideas *into* the text (this is the bad way to read).
- **Genre:** The style of literature a book is written in (poetry, history, letter, prophecy).

Precision Note (grown-up wording): Hermeneutics is the science and art of biblical interpretation, focused on discovering the author's original intent.

Bible Receipts

The Bible itself tells us that studying Scripture requires hard work and careful handling.

Paul warned Timothy that sloppy theology destroys people. He commanded him: "Be diligent to present yourself to God as one approved, a worker who doesn't need to be ashamed, correctly teaching the word of truth" (2 Timothy 2:15, CSB).

Notice the words *diligent* and *worker*. Reading the Bible correctly isn't magic. It takes effort. You have to handle it carefully, like a surgeon with a scalpel, not a toddler with a chainsaw.

In the Old Testament, after the Israelites returned from exile, the priest Ezra gathered the people to read the Scriptures to them. But he didn't just read the words and walk away. Nehemiah 8:8 (CSB) says, "They read out of the book of the law of God, translating and giving the meaning so that the people could understand what was read."

They gave the meaning. They explained the context. God doesn't want you to just stare at words on a page; He wants your mind to actively understand what the original author was communicating.

Truth in Plain English

To stop twisting the Bible, you just need to stop reading it like a magic 8-ball.

You can't just close your eyes, flip your Bible open to a random page, point your finger, and say, "God, give me a sign for today." The Bible is a library of historical books, not a fortune cookie.

Every time you read a passage, you need to ask three vital questions:

1. *What did this mean to the original audience?*
2. *What is the timeless truth about God in this passage?*
3. *How does this apply to my life today?*

Highlightable line: The Bible was written *for* you, but it was not originally written *to* you.

If you read a letter Paul wrote to the church in Corinth, you are reading someone else's mail. You have to understand what was happening in their city before you can apply Paul's advice to your high school.

Common Confusion Box

Confusion #1: "The Holy Spirit will just tell me what it means in my heart." This sounds right because the Holy Spirit absolutely illuminates our minds to understand God's word. But it's wrong. The Holy Spirit will never bypass your brain to give you a "secret meaning" that contradicts the original text. The Spirit's job isn't to help you ignore context; His job is to help you submit to the truth the context reveals.

Highlightable line: If your interpretation of a verse completely ignores the verses around it, your interpretation is wrong.

Confusion #2: "Well, that's what the verse means to me." This sounds right because our culture tells us that truth is subjective and based entirely on personal feelings. But here is what Scripture shows instead: God is the author, which means God holds the copyright on the meaning. A verse means exactly what God intended it to mean, regardless of how it makes you feel. Your job is to discover His meaning, not invent your own.

Why This Changes Real Life

When you learn to read the Bible in context, the pressure comes off.

You don't have to be a seminary professor, and you don't have to wait for a mystical, emotional chill down your spine every time you open the pages. You just need to be a careful reader.

Think about the confidence this gives you. When a celebrity or a TikTok influencer uses a Bible verse to justify something that feels incredibly wrong, you don't have to be intimidated by them. You can calmly open the chapter, look at the surrounding verses, and see the truth for yourself.

Context turns the Bible from a confusing rulebook into a massive, gorgeous landscape. When you see how the geography, the history, and the surrounding verses connect, the Bible stops feeling boring. It becomes the most gripping, intense, and deeply moving book you've ever read.

Highlightable line: Good theology doesn't kill your passion; it gives your passion a solid place to stand.

Try This This Week

The "Zoom Out" Test. Pick a famous, bumper-sticker Bible verse (like Jeremiah 29:11). Before you claim it for your own life, read the entire chapter surrounding it. Find out who was talking, who they were talking to, and what was happening in history at that exact moment. Write down one detail from the context that completely changes the meaning of that single verse.

Talk It Out

- Have you ever seen someone use a Bible verse out of context to prove a point? What happened?
- Why is it so tempting to skip the hard work of context and just jump straight to "what this means to me"?
- How does treating the Bible like a magic 8-ball actually disrespect God?
- If Paul wrote Philippians 4:13 while facing execution in a filthy prison, how does that change the way you can use this verse when you are having a terrible day?

BELIEF BUILDER (Brick #2: About the Bible)

My one-sentence belief: "I believe I must read the Bible carefully and in context to discover what God actually meant."

Bible receipts (pick 1–2): 2 Timothy 2:15; Nehemiah 8:8

This changes my life because: "It protects me from being manipulated by false teaching and helps me hear God's true voice."

One question I still have: (Write one honest question. No pretending.)

Short Prayer

Father, protect me from twisting Your words to fit my agenda. Jesus, give me a deep desire to study the Scriptures carefully. Holy Spirit, open my eyes to see the original meaning behind every text. Make me a diligent worker. Keep me from settling for shallow, out-of-context answers. Amen.

My Notes & Thoughts

Brick #3: The Big Story of the Bible

Cold Open Moment

Imagine walking into a movie theater halfway through a film.

You sit down, grab some popcorn, and look at the screen. A massive battle is happening. Explosions are going off. The main character is crying. The villain is laughing.

You're watching the movie, but you have no idea what is actually going on. You don't know why the hero is fighting, what the stakes are, or who betrayed who in the first act. You are witnessing the action, but because you missed the beginning of the story, the current moment makes zero sense.

This is exactly how most people experience the Bible.

We drop in to read a random Psalm, or we listen to a sermon about David and Goliath, or we read a weird story in Genesis about a guy building a giant boat. We look at these isolated scenes, and we try to extract a quick moral lesson for our day.

But if you don't know the overarching storyline, if you don't know what happened in Act 1, or where the whole thing is heading in Act 4, the Bible will constantly feel like a confusing mess of disconnected rules and weird ancient stories.

Big Idea

The Bible isn't a random collection of moral fables; it is one unified story of God rescuing a broken world through Jesus.

Why This Matters

If you miss the big story of the Bible, you will inevitably make the Bible about *you*.

You will read the story of David and Goliath and think, "I am David, and my math test is Goliath, and God wants me to win." But the Bible isn't about you slaying your personal giants. It's about Jesus slaying the giants of sin and death.

- **It gives your life a setting.** You aren't just floating randomly through history; you are living inside God's unfolding epic.

- **It makes sense of the suffering.** When you know the ending of the story, you can survive the brutal middle chapters.

Key Words

- **Metanarrative:** The overarching, grand storyline that connects all the smaller stories together.
- **Creation:** God making the world perfectly good and humans in His image.
- **Fall:** Humanity rebelling against God, bringing sin, death, and brokenness into the world.
- **Redemption:** God's mission to rescue sinners and buy them back through the death and resurrection of Jesus.
- **Restoration:** The future promise that Jesus will return to destroy evil completely and make the heavens and earth new.

Precision Note (grown-up wording): Redemptive History (or *Heilsgeschichte*) is the framework for understanding all of Scripture as the unfolding plan of God's salvation culminating in Christ.

Bible Receipts

After Jesus rose from the dead, He was walking with two of His followers on the road to Emmaus. They were confused and discouraged. They knew the Old Testament stories, but they didn't understand how Jesus' death fit into them.

So Jesus stopped and gave them the greatest Bible study in history. "Then beginning with Moses and all the Prophets, he interpreted for them the things concerning himself in all the Scriptures" (Luke 24:27, CSB).

Jesus boldly claimed that the *entire* Old Testament, the law, the prophets, the weird stories, the kings, the sacrifices, was fundamentally about Him. He is the main character of the whole book.

The Apostle Paul confirms where this massive story is headed. He writes about God's grand plan in Colossians 1:19-20 (CSB): "For God was pleased to have all his fullness dwell in him 'Jesus.'

, and through him to reconcile everything to himself, whether things on earth or things in heaven, by making peace through his blood, shed on the cross."

The story started with God creating everything perfectly, and the story will end with God reconciling everything perfectly through the cross.

Truth in Plain English

The Bible is a library of 66 books, but it tells one story in four massive acts: Creation, Fall, Redemption, and Restoration.

Act 1: Creation. God made a perfect world. There was no cancer, no betrayal, no anxiety, and no death. Humans lived in perfect friendship with God.

Act 2: Fall. Humans decided they wanted to be the boss instead of God. They rebelled, and this shattered the world.

Sin infected the human heart, and death entered the universe. Every piece of pain you have ever felt traces back to this act.

Act 3: Redemption. God didn't abandon us. He immediately launched a rescue mission.

The entire Old Testament tracks this mission through the nation of Israel, leading directly to the birth, life, death, and resurrection of Jesus. Jesus takes the punishment for the Fall, breaking the back of sin and death.

Act 4: Restoration. Jesus is coming back, and when He does, He won't just take us away to float on clouds. He is going to purge evil from the earth and restore the universe to its original, perfect design.

Highlightable line: You don't have to carry the weight of the world; you just have to trust the King who holds the story.

Right now, you and I are living right in the middle of the tension. Act 3 has happened (Jesus saved us), but Act 4 hasn't fully arrived yet (the world is still broken).

Common Confusion Box

Confusion #1: "The Old Testament is about a mean, angry God, and the New Testament is about a nice, loving Jesus." This sounds right because the Old Testament has lots of judgment, fire, and rules, while Jesus talks a lot about love and grace. But it's wrong. It's the exact same God telling the exact same story. The Old Testament is packed with God's extreme patience and mercy toward rebellious Israel. And the New Testament? Jesus talks about hell and final judgment more than anyone else in the Bible. God has always been perfectly holy and perfectly loving in both Testaments.

Highlightable line: The Bible isn't a book of random heroes to copy; it is a book about one Hero coming to save us all.

Confusion #2: "The Bible is just an instruction manual for life." This sounds right because there are plenty of commands in Scripture about how to live well. But here is what Scripture shows instead: if the Bible is just a manual, then Christianity is just about you performing well. But the Bible is a rescue story. Instructions tell you what to do; a rescue story tells you what has already been done for you.

Why This Changes Real Life

When you finally see the grand metanarrative (Creation, Fall, Redemption, Restoration), everything about your daily life clicks into place.

It explains why the world is so beautiful and why you love sunsets and friendship, because of Creation. It explains why the world is so vicious, why people get sick, and why friends stab you in the back, because of the Fall.

Redemption explains why you don't have to constantly earn your way into God's love. And Restoration explains why you can have deep, unbreakable hope, even when you are standing at the grave of someone you love.

You aren't a cosmic accident. You are a character written into the most important story in the universe, and the Author of the story loves you enough to die for you.

Highlightable line: Knowing the end of the story gives you the courage to survive the middle.

Try This This Week

Grab a sticky note and write the letters **C - F - RE - RO** (Creation, Fall, Redemption, Restoration) on it. Stick it on your bathroom mirror. Every morning this week, point to the letters and remind yourself: "The world is broken (F), but Jesus paid for my sins (RE), and He is coming back to fix everything (RO)."

Talk It Out

- Which of the four acts (Creation, Fall, Redemption, Restoration) do you think about the most? Which one do you think about the least?
- Why is it dangerous to read Old Testament stories as if they are just fables about how to be a "good person"?
- How does living in the tension between Redemption (Act 3) and Restoration (Act 4) explain why Christians still experience suffering and doubt?
- If Jesus is the main character of the whole Bible, how should that change the way we read it?

BELIEF BUILDER (Brick #3: About the Bible)

My one-sentence belief: "I believe the Bible tells one unified story of God creating the world, humanity breaking it, and Jesus coming to rescue and restore it."

Bible receipts (pick 1–2): Luke 24:27; Colossians 1:19–20

This changes my life because: "It reminds me that my life is not a random accident, but part of God's massive rescue mission."

One question I still have: (Write one honest question. No pretending.)

Short Prayer

Father, thank You for authoring a story that ends in ultimate victory. Jesus, thank You for stepping into our broken world to be the Hero we could never be. Holy Spirit, help me to see Jesus on every page of Scripture. When I am discouraged by the brokenness of the Fall, remind me of the hope of Restoration. Let my life bring glory to Your great story. Amen.

My Notes & Thoughts

PART 1 - CHECKPOINT

Assemble Your First Statement Section: "About the Bible"

You made it through Part 1. You've laid the foundation. Now it's time to stop reading and start building.

At the end of the last three chapters, you wrote down three "bricks" (your one-sentence beliefs). Right now, they are just scattered pieces. In this checkpoint, you are going to cement them together into a clean, powerful paragraph that will become the first official section of your Personal Statement of Faith.

Step 1: Gather Your Bricks

Look back at the Belief Builder sections from Chapters 1, 2, and 3. Write all three of your one-sentence beliefs right here:

- **Brick 1 (Authority):** ______________________________
- **Brick 2 (Interpretation):** ______________________________
- **Brick 3 (The Big Story):** ______________________________

Step 2: Edit for Power

Right now, your sentences might sound a little clunky or repetitive. That's okay. Real theology takes editing.

Look at your three sentences and apply the **"Red Pen Rules"**:

1. **Cross out filler words.** (Remove phrases like "I just think," "basically," or "stuff.")
2. **Circle duplicates.** (If you used the phrase "word of God" three times, keep the best one and change the others.)
3. **Upgrade your vocabulary.** (If you wrote, "God made sure the writers didn't mess up," cross it out and use your precision words: "The Bible is the *inspired* and *inerrant* word of God.")

Step 3: Draft Your Official Paragraph

Now, combine your edited bricks into one flowing paragraph. It should be 3–4 sentences maximum. It needs to sound like *you*, but a very confident, anchored version of you. There is space for you to write at the end of this chapter.

My Statement of Faith: ABOUT THE BIBLE

(Example Draft: "I believe the Bible is the inspired, inerrant word of God, completely true and totally trustworthy. It must be read carefully and in its original context to understand God's true voice. It is not a collection of random rules, but one unified story of God creating the world, humanity breaking it, and Jesus coming to rescue and restore it.")

Step 4: The 10-Second Spoken Test

Your Personal Statement of Faith isn't just for a piece of paper; it's for real life. If a friend asks you what you believe about the Bible in the hallway between classes, you can't read them a four-sentence paragraph. You need a fast, sharp answer.

Look at your drafted paragraph and condense it into a single, spoken sentence that takes less than 10 seconds to say out loud.

My 10-Second Spoken Script:

"I believe the Bible is God's true word, and it tells the true story of how Jesus came to rescue a broken world."

Read your 10-second script out loud right now. Does it sound natural? Does it sound confident? If you stumbled, tweak the words until it flows easily off your tongue.

Step 5: Log Your Receipts

A statement of faith without Scripture is just an opinion. Pick the **two strongest Bible verses** from Part 1 that back up your new paragraph, and write the references here so you don't lose them.

1. ________________________________ (Example: 2 Timothy 3:16-17)
2. ________________________________ (Example: Luke 24:27)

Congratulations. You just built the first major pillar of your theology. You are ready for Part 2.

<u>My Statement of Faith (after part 1)</u>

PART 2 - GOD: WHO HE IS

In this part, we're going straight to the center: **who God is.** Not a "bigger human," not a cosmic vibe, God as the Bible actually reveals Him. We'll explore God's character, why His holiness and love belong together, and why the Trinity isn't cringe or nonsense, it's the best news about God's heart. The goal here is simple: you'll build a clear "About God" section for your Statement of Faith that you can actually say out loud, and you'll start forming the kind of view of God that steadies you when life feels chaotic.

Brick #4: God Is Not a Bigger Human

Cold Open Moment

Think about how you usually picture God in your head.

If you are really honest, you probably imagine someone who operates a lot like you do, just on a massive scale. When you get frustrated with someone, you assume God is up in heaven rolling His eyes at them, too. When you feel overwhelmed by your schedule, you picture God frantically trying to manage eight billion prayers at once, hoping He doesn't drop the ball.

We do this because humans are the highest form of life we can see. So, we project our own human traits onto God. We think of Him like a Marvel superhero, a guy with a booming voice, a really nice beard, and unlimited superpowers.

But treating God like a bigger, stronger version of yourself is actually incredibly dangerous.

If God is just a super-sized human, then He has human limitations. He gets tired. He gets stressed. He has to learn new things. And a God who gets stressed out is not a God who can save you.

Big Idea

God is the Creator, which means He is entirely different from everything He has created; He is not a bigger version of you.

Why This Matters

This is the starting line for knowing who God actually is.

If you get this wrong, your prayer life will be a wreck. You will constantly try to negotiate with God, assuming you can explain your situation to Him in a way He hasn't thought of yet.

- **It kills your anxiety.** If God isn't human, He doesn't panic when your life falls apart.
- **It restores your awe.** You can't worship someone who is basically just your imaginary peer.

Key Words

- **Creator:** The one who made everything out of nothing. God existed before time, space, and matter.
- **Creature:** Anything that was made by God (including humans, angels, and the universe).
- **Omniscient:** God knows everything. He never has to learn, guess, or google anything.
- **Omnipotent:** God has all power to do whatever He decides to do.

Precision Note (grown-up wording): Theologians talk about the *Creator-creature distinction*, meaning God has *incommunicable attributes* (traits that belong only to Him, like being everywhere at once) that humans do not share.

Bible Receipts

The Bible goes out of its way to aggressively remind us that God is not in our category.

Look at what God says through the prophet Isaiah: "For my thoughts are not your thoughts, and your ways are not my ways. This is the LORD's declaration. For as heaven is higher than earth, so my ways are higher than your ways, and my thoughts than your thoughts" (Isaiah 55:8-9, CSB).

God is essentially saying, "Stop assuming you know how my mind works." His logic, His timeline, and His decisions operate on a level we can't fully grasp.

In Psalm 50, God confronts people who were treating Him casually. He lists their sins, their hypocrisy, and their fake religion, and then He hits them with a devastating line.

"You have done these things, and I kept silent; you thought I was just like you. But I will rebuke you and lay out the case before you" (Psalm 50:21, CSB).

You thought I was just like you. That is the ultimate insult to the Creator. We cannot drag God down to our level.

Truth in Plain English

Here is what it means that God is not a bigger human.

First, God doesn't have bad days. He never wakes up on the wrong side of the bed. His mood doesn't fluctuate based on whether or not you read your Bible today. He is entirely consistent.

Second, God never learns anything. Has that ever crossed your mind? Nothing has ever occurred to God. He has never said, "Oh wow, I didn't see that coming!" He knows the end from the beginning perfectly.

Highlightable line: You never have to catch God up on the details of your life; He already knows the things you are too scared to say out loud.

Third, God doesn't get exhausted. You have limits. You need eight hours of sleep and a meal or you completely fall apart. God doesn't require a battery recharge. He sustains the entire universe without breaking a sweat.

Common Confusion Box

Confusion #1: "If God isn't human-like, then He can't possibly understand what I'm going through." This sounds right because we usually want advice from someone who has been in our exact shoes. We think an infinite God must be cold, distant, and disconnected from our teenage drama. But it's wrong. Because God created you, He understands the mechanics of your heart better than you do. And more importantly, God the Son actually *did* step into our world and become a human in the person of Jesus. He knows exactly what tears, betrayal, and pain feel like.

Highlightable line: God's infinite power doesn't make Him distant; it makes Him capable of handling your heaviest burdens.

Confusion #2: "But the Bible says God has 'hands' and 'eyes'." This sounds right because verses talk about God's "strong right hand" or His "eyes roaming the earth." But here is what Scripture shows instead: The Bible is using human language to help our tiny brains understand infinite truths (theologians call this *anthropomorphism*). God is spirit. He doesn't have physical eyeballs. The writers are just using a metaphor to say, "God sees everything."

Why This Changes Real Life

Realizing God isn't a bigger human is the ultimate cure for control freaks.

When you go through a massive life transition, like graduating, dealing with a breakup, or watching your family move to a new city, it feels terrifying because you don't know what is going to happen next. Your human limitations are suddenly very obvious.

If your God is just a bigger human, you will panic. You will try to micromanage your life, manipulate your friends, and force things to go your way.

But when you realize your God is the omniscient, omnipotent Creator of the universe, you can exhale. You can stop trying to play God. You don't have to hold the universe together, because the One who does has never dropped it.

Highlightable line: You can finally rest when you realize the universe already has a CEO, and nobody is asking for your resume.

Try This This Week

The "I Don't Know" exercise. Sometime this week, when you feel completely stressed out about a situation, pull out your phone and type this in your notes app: *"God, I have absolutely no idea how to fix this, but You do."* Acknowledge your human limitation, and acknowledge His divine unlimitedness.

Talk It Out

- What is a human emotion or reaction that you frequently (and maybe accidentally) project onto God?
- Why do you think the phrase "You thought I was just like you" is considered a massive insult to God?
- How does knowing that God *never learns anything new* change the way you pray to Him?
- What is one area of your life where you are currently trying to "play God" by controlling everything?

BELIEF BUILDER (Brick #4: About God)

My one-sentence belief: "I believe God is the infinite Creator of all things, and He does not share my human limitations."

Bible receipts (pick 1–2): Isaiah 55:8–9; Psalm 50:21

This changes my life because: "I can stop trying to control everything and trust the God who actually knows the future."

One question I still have: (Write one honest question. No pretending.)

Short Prayer

Father, forgive me for making You so small in my mind. Jesus, thank You for showing me the exact image of the invisible God. Holy Spirit, remind me of my limits today so I can lean on Your limitless power. When I try to play God, gently knock me off the throne. Help me rest in the fact that You are completely in charge. Amen.

My Notes & Thoughts

—•—

Brick #5: God Is Holy (and why that's good)

Cold Open Moment

When you hear the word "holy," what picture pops into your head?

Usually, it's not a great one. We tend to associate "holy" with things that are painfully boring or overly strict. You might picture a dusty church building, a choir singing a slow song you don't know the words to, or a youth pastor telling you to stop having fun.

In our modern vocabulary, being "holy" basically means being a buzzkill. It means you are the person who doesn't laugh at the joke, never goes to the party, and constantly points out everyone else's flaws.

So when the Bible tells us that God is holy, we subconsciously wince.

We imagine God as the ultimate cosmic principal, walking the hallways of the universe with a clipboard, looking for rule-breakers to send to detention. We think His holiness means He is irritated with us. But if that is your definition of holiness, you are missing out on the most beautiful, breathtaking thing about who God is.

Big Idea

God's holiness means He is completely set apart and flawlessly pure; He is dangerously good.

Why This Matters

If God is not perfectly holy, you have a massive problem.

Think about human politicians, celebrities, or leaders. Even the best ones eventually compromise. They get bought off, they tell white lies, or they cover up their mistakes to protect their reputation. If God isn't absolutely holy, it means He could be corrupted. It means He could lie to you, change His mind, or treat you unfairly just because He feels like it.

- **It guarantees justice.** A holy God cannot be bribed, and He will not sweep evil under the rug.
- **It gives you a standard.** Without God's holiness, "right" and "wrong" are just opinions made up by culture.

Key Words

- **Holy:** Literally means to be "set apart" or cut off from everything else. It means God is uniquely separate from creation and completely free from sin.
- **Purity:** Having absolutely zero flaws, evil, or dark motives.
- **Glory:** The visible, heavy, beautiful weight of God's holiness on display.

- **Awe:** The feeling of profound respect mixed with a healthy dose of fear when you encounter something infinitely bigger than you.

Precision Note (grown-up wording): Theologians refer to God's *transcendence*, meaning He is exalted far above the created universe and exists in a realm of absolute moral perfection.

Bible Receipts

When humans in the Bible actually encounter God's holiness, they never yawn. They usually drop to the floor in terror.

In Isaiah 6, the prophet gets a vision of God sitting on His throne. The angels around God aren't singing about His love or His patience. They are shaking the building by screaming, "Holy, holy, holy is the LORD of Armies; his glory fills the whole earth" (Isaiah 6:3, CSB).

In Hebrew, repeating a word three times is the ultimate way to emphasize it. It's the highest possible superlative. God isn't just holy; He is holy, holy, holy.

Isaiah's response wasn't to take a selfie. He panicked. "Woe is me for I am ruined because I am a man of unclean lips" (Isaiah 6:5, CSB). Staring at God's absolute purity instantly exposed Isaiah's absolute sinfulness.

But this holiness isn't just for God to keep to Himself. The Apostle Peter writes to the early Christians and says, "But as the one who called you is holy, you also are to be holy in all your conduct; for it is written, Be holy, because I am holy" (1 Peter 1:15-16, CSB).

God expects His people to reflect His family resemblance.

Truth in Plain English

Holiness isn't a boring list of rules; it is blazing, radiant perfection.

Think of God's holiness like the sun. The sun is incredibly good. It provides light, warmth, and life to the entire planet. But the sun is also incredibly dangerous. If you try to stare directly into it, it will blind you. If you fly too close to it, it will incinerate you.

Highlightable line: God's holiness doesn't mean He hates you; it means He is so pure that sin cannot survive in His presence.

God doesn't do good things because He is checking off a moral to-do list. He does good things because He *is* good. He can no more tell a lie or act selfishly than a flashlight can shoot out darkness.

Because He is entirely pure, He is the safest being in the universe to trust with your life. He will never use you, manipulate you, or betray you.

Common Confusion Box

Confusion #1: "God's holiness means He is just waiting to punish me." This sounds right because if God is perfectly pure, and we are constantly messing up, we assume His default reaction must be to strike us with lightning. But it's wrong. God's holiness demands that sin be punished, but God's love provided the substitute. Jesus took the blazing heat of God's holy justice on the cross so that we wouldn't have to.

Highlightable line: God was so holy He couldn't ignore your sin, but He was so loving He refused to let you pay for it alone.

Confusion #2: "Being holy just means dressing nicely and not swearing." This sounds right because for a long time, church culture reduced "holiness" to behavioral management, mostly focusing on clothes, language, and movies. But here is what

Scripture shows instead: True holiness starts in the heart, not the wardrobe. You can follow every conservative rule in the world and still have a heart full of pride, racism, and bitterness. God's holiness transforms you from the inside out.

Why This Changes Real Life

When you grasp the holiness of God, you stop treating Him casually.

We live in a culture that treats everything as a joke. We meme our trauma, we mock our leaders, and we are cynical about literally everything. We often drag that same casual attitude into church. We treat God like He is our celestial buddy or a cosmic vending machine.

But a clear view of God's holiness kills our pride.

When you realize the Creator of the universe is blazing with absolute perfection, it changes the way you talk to Him. It makes your worship deeper. You stop complaining about why God isn't doing what you want, and you start standing in awe that a God this holy would even know your name.

Highlightable line: A casual view of God will leave you with a fragile faith; an awe-filled view of God will give you a faith of steel.

Try This This Week

The "Screen Time" Audit. God calls you to reflect His holiness. Take a five-minute scroll through your most-used social media app, your recent text messages, or the last three shows you watched. Ask yourself: *Does the content I am feeding my brain reflect the purity of a holy God, or the toxic noise of a broken world?* ### Talk It Out

- If you had to describe what "holy" meant to someone who had never been to church, what would you say?
- Why do you think Isaiah's immediate reaction to seeing God was to panic about his own sin?
- How does viewing God's holiness like the sun (good but dangerously powerful) change how you approach Him?
- What is the difference between true biblical holiness and just being a "good, religious person"?

BELIEF BUILDER (Brick #5: About God)

My one-sentence belief: "I believe God is perfectly holy, completely set apart, and entirely pure in everything He does."

Bible receipts (pick 1–2): Isaiah 6:3–5; 1 Peter 1:15–16

This changes my life because: "It gives me a perfect standard of goodness and reminds me to treat God with deep awe and respect."

One question I still have: (Write one honest question. No pretending.)

Short Prayer

Father, You are holy, holy, holy. Jesus, thank You for perfectly fulfilling the holy standard I could never reach. Holy Spirit, burn away the impurity in my life and make me more like You. Forgive me for treating Your name casually. Restore my awe and wonder at who You are. Amen.

My Notes & Thoughts

Brick #6: God Is Love (not soft)

Cold Open Moment

We have absolutely ruined the word *love.*

We use it for everything. You love your mom. You love your dog. You love that new song on Spotify. You love double-stuffed Oreos. Because we use the same word to describe our affection for a parent and our affection for a cookie, the word has lost almost all of its weight.

So when a youth pastor stands on a stage and says, "God loves you," it often bounces right off of us. It sounds like a warm, fuzzy greeting card.

Even worse, our culture has redefined "love" to mean absolute, uncritical approval. We are told that if someone truly loves you, they will never tell you that you are wrong. They will just affirm whatever you want to do.

If we drag that definition of love onto God, we end up with a God who acts like a weak, overly permissive grandparent. A God who just smiles, hands out candy, and lets you run into traffic because He doesn't want to hurt your feelings.

But that isn't love. That is just being soft. And God is not soft.

Big Idea

God doesn't just do loving things; He is the very definition of love, and His love is fiercely committed to your ultimate good.

Why This Matters

If you misunderstand God's love, you will run away from Him the second He tells you "no."

If you think love means getting everything you want, you will assume God hates you when He allows you to go through a breakup, fail a test, or face consequences for a bad choice.

- **It anchors your identity.** When you know God's love is tough and real, you stop trying to earn approval from people who don't actually care about you.
- **It redefines your boundaries.** You realize God's rules aren't meant to restrict your joy; they are meant to protect it.

Key Words

- **Agape:** The Greek word for the highest form of love. It is a choice to sacrificially seek the ultimate good of another person, regardless of how you feel.
- **Grace:** God giving us incredible gifts (like salvation) that we absolutely do not deserve.
- **Mercy:** God withholding the terrible punishment that we actually do deserve.
- **Righteousness:** Acting in perfect alignment with what is right, just, and true.

Precision Note (grown-up wording): Theologians speak of *Divine Simplicity*, meaning God is not a collection of conflicting parts. His love and His justice are not at war; He is entirely loving and entirely just at the exact same time.

Bible Receipts

The Apostle John makes one of the most staggering claims in the entire Bible.

He doesn't just say God has a lot of love, or that God acts lovingly. He writes, "The one who does not love does not know God, because God is love" (1 John 4:8, CSB).

Love isn't just an activity God does; it is His essence. It is who He is. But John immediately defines what this love actually looks like in the real world.

"God's love was revealed among us in this way: God sent his one and only Son into the world so that we might live through him. Love consists in this: not that we loved God, but that he loved us and sent his Son to be the atoning sacrifice for our sins" (1 John 4:9-10, CSB).

Highlightable line: Biblical love isn't a feeling in your chest; it is a bloody cross on a hill.

The Apostle Paul backs this up. He wants to prove that God's love isn't based on our good behavior. "But God proves his own love for us in that while we were still sinners, Christ died for us" (Romans 5:8, CSB).

God didn't wait for you to clean yourself up before He loved you. He loved you at your absolute worst.

Truth in Plain English

Here is the difference between cultural love and God's love.

Cultural love says, "I love you because you are awesome, and I will support anything that makes you happy." God's love says, "I love you despite your sin, and I care about you too much to let you stay the way you are."

Imagine you have a friend who is addicted to dangerous drugs. If you practice cultural "love," you will give them money to buy more drugs because you want them to be happy in the moment. But if you practice real *agape* love, you will flush their drugs down the toilet, endure their screaming, and drive them to rehab.

Real love is fiercely protective. Real love is willing to be the bad guy in the short term for the sake of the other person's long-term survival.

Highlightable line: God will never sacrifice your ultimate holiness for the sake of your temporary happiness.

Because God is love, He hates anything that destroys the people He loves. His love is entirely compatible with His anger toward sin.

Common Confusion Box

Confusion #1: "If God really loves me, my life should be easier." This sounds right because we equate love with comfort. We assume a loving God would clear all the obstacles out of our path. But it's wrong. The Bible says the exact opposite. Hebrews 12:6 says, "For the Lord disciplines the one he loves." Just like a good coach pushes an athlete through painful drills to make them stronger, God allows us to go through suffering to mature our faith. Pain is not proof that God stopped loving you.

Highlightable line: God's love is not a guarantee of an easy life; it is a guarantee of His presence in a hard one.

Confusion #2: "I have to do good things so God will love me more." This sounds right because every other relationship in our lives works this way. You have to earn a spot on the team, earn your grades, and earn your friends' respect. But here is what Scripture shows instead: God's love for you is not tied to your performance. He loves you perfectly right now. You cannot make Him love you more by reading your Bible, and you cannot make Him love you less by failing a test or messing up.

Why This Changes Real Life

Understanding the fierce, unchanging love of God is the only way to get off the emotional roller coaster.

Right now, you probably evaluate your worth based on your performance. If you get a lot of likes on a post, score a goal, or get a compliment, you feel lovable. If you get ignored, fail an exam, or get ghosted by a friend, you feel completely worthless.

When you anchor your life to God's *agape* love, that toxic cycle stops.

You realize that the Creator of the universe looked at your darkest thoughts, your worst habits, and your deepest failures, and He chose to die for you anyway. You are entirely known, and you are entirely loved.

When that reality sinks into your bones, you become incredibly brave. You don't have to be crushed by a bully's insult, because their opinion of you doesn't define your worth. God's love does.

Try This This Week

The "Even When" exercise. Write down three things you are deeply ashamed of (a specific sin, a failure, or an insecurity). Next to each one, write the phrase: *"Even when I [insert failure], God still perfectly loves me."* Read it, rip the paper up, and throw it in the trash as a reminder that your performance does not dictate His love.

Talk It Out

- How does the world's definition of "love" differ from the biblical definition of *agape*?
- Why is it actually unloving to simply affirm whatever someone wants to do?
- Read Romans 5:8 again. Why is it important that God loved us *while we were still sinners*, instead of waiting for us to get better?
- How does knowing God's love is fierce (like a coach or a surgeon) change the way you view the hard seasons of your life?

BELIEF BUILDER (Brick #6: About God)

My one-sentence belief: "I believe God is perfect love, and His love is fiercely committed to my ultimate good, not just my temporary comfort."

Bible receipts (pick 1–2): 1 John 4:8–10; Romans 5:8

This changes my life because: "I don't have to earn my worth through performance; I am completely known and perfectly loved by God."

One question I still have: (Write one honest question. No pretending.)

Short Prayer

Father, thank You for loving me when I was completely unlovable. Jesus, thank You for proving Your love with Your life and Your cross. Holy Spirit, pour the reality of God's love so deeply into my heart that I stop seeking approval from others. When I think love is just a soft feeling, remind me of Your fierce commitment to my good. Amen.

My Notes & Thoughts

Brick #7: The Trinity Without the Cringe

Cold Open Moment

You know how this usually happens. You are in a conversation, and someone drops a line that sounds confident enough to shut the whole discussion down.

'Three in one? That's not deep theology. That's just bad math.'

In the moment, you don't have a clean response. So you do the safe thing: you smile, shrug, or toss out the classic church line, "Well, it's just a mystery", and hope nobody asks a follow-up question. But later, their comment sticks with you. Because if the Trinity is just math that doesn't work, then Christianity is built on nonsense.

And if the Trinity *is* true, then God isn't a lonely power sitting in the sky. It means God isn't a solo Person who needed to create humans just so He'd have someone to love.

It means love didn't begin when creation began. Love has always been real, because God has always been Father, Son, and Spirit. That's not a confusing side detail. That's the center of the entire universe.

Big Idea

God is one God in three Persons, Father, Son, and Holy Spirit, and that is the absolute best news about who God is.

Why This Matters

You might be thinking, "Okay, but why should I care? Can't I just love Jesus and skip the confusing math?"

No, because this changes the ground under your feet. If you get God wrong, everything else gets wobbly, your prayer life, your worship, your salvation, and even how you define love.

If God is just a single, isolated being, He didn't know what love was until He created angels or humans. That would mean He needed us to feel complete. But because the Trinity is true, perfect relationship has always existed inside who God is. He didn't create you because He was lonely and desperate for a friend; He created you to invite you into the massive love that already existed.

Key Words

- **Trinity:** The truth that God is one in essence, but exists eternally as three distinct Persons (Father, Son, and Holy Spirit).
- **Person:** Not a human person with a physical body, but a real "Who" within God. The Father is a Who, the Son is a Who, and the Spirit is a Who.
- **Essence:** The "What" of God. There is only one divine nature, and all three Persons share it completely.

Precision Note (grown-up wording): Theologians say God is one in *essence* (homoousios) but three in *person* (hypostasis).

Bible Receipts

The word "Trinity" isn't actually in the Bible, but the reality of the Trinity is smeared across almost every page.

Look at the baptism of Jesus. "When Jesus was baptized, he went up immediately from the water. The heavens suddenly opened for him, and he saw the Spirit of God descending like a dove and coming down on him. And a voice from heaven said, 'This is my beloved Son, with whom I am well-pleased'" (Matthew 3:16-17, CSB).

All three Persons are active at the exact same moment. The Father is speaking from heaven. The Son is standing in the water. The Spirit is descending like a dove.

Now look at the massive final command Jesus gives His followers before leaving earth. 'Go, therefore, and make disciples of all nations, baptizing them in the name of the Father and of the Son and of the Holy Spirit' (Matthew 28:19, CSB). Notice He uses the word 'name' (singular), not 'names' (plural). It is one name, shared equally by three Persons.

Truth in Plain English

The easiest way to understand the Trinity without breaking your brain is to remember the difference between "What" and "Who."

You are one "what" (a human) and one "who" (your name). God is completely different from us. God is one "What" (the divine Creator) but three "Whos" (Father, Son, and Spirit).

Highlightable line: The Father is God, the Son is God, and the Spirit is God, but the Father is not the Son, and the Son is not the Spirit.

The Father plans salvation. The Son accomplishes salvation on the cross. The Spirit applies that salvation to your heart today. They are not three gods competing for the spotlight. They are one God, working in perfect, unbroken harmony.

Common Confusion Box

Confusion #1: 'The Trinity is like an egg (shell, white, yolk) or water (ice, liquid, gas).' This sounds right because well-meaning Sunday school teachers have used these analogies for decades to try and make a massive concept simple. But it's wrong. An egg is divided into three parts, but God is not sliced into thirds (that is a heresy called *Partialism*). Water changes forms depending on the temperature, but God doesn't change masks or switch modes between being the Father, Son, and Spirit (that is a heresy called *Modalism*). Ultimately, every human analogy breaks down because God is entirely unique.

Highlightable line: You don't have to fully comprehend God to completely trust Him; if you could fit God inside your brain, He wouldn't be big enough to worship.

Confusion #2: "Christians actually believe in three different gods." This sounds right to people outside of Christianity because praying to the Father, the Son, and the Spirit sounds like a committee. But here is what Scripture shows instead: Christianity is fiercely monotheistic (believing in one God). Deuteronomy 6:4 says, "Listen, Israel: The LORD our God, the LORD is one." We don't worship a committee. We worship one infinite God who exists eternally as three Persons.

Why This Changes Real Life

When you grasp the Trinity, it radically transforms the way you pray.

You aren't just shouting into the void, hoping a distant boss hears you. You are actually praying *to* the Father, *through* the work of the Son, *by* the power of the Holy Spirit. You are caught up in the middle of a divine relationship.

It should also bring you massive comfort when you feel isolated. The Holy Spirit living inside of you is the exact same God who spoke the universe into existence. Jesus, who advocates for you to the Father, is the exact same God who knows the number of hairs on your head. You are never, ever alone.

Highlightable line: You don't earn your way into God's love; because of the Trinity, you are simply invited into the love that has always been there.

Try This This Week

For the next 7 days, try praying this Trinitarian prayer once a day, out loud if you can: *Father, thank You for making me and caring for me. Jesus, thank You for saving me and staying with me. Holy Spirit, help me follow You today.*

Talk It Out

- What part is hardest for you to hold together in your mind: the "one God" part or the "three Persons" part?
- Why do you think people (even in the church) try to avoid talking about the Trinity?
- Look at the "Common Confusion" box. What is a popular analogy you've heard about the Trinity, and how does it actually fail?
- If someone asked you tomorrow, "What is the Trinity?" what is your 10-second answer?

BELIEF BUILDER (Brick #7: About God)

My one-sentence belief: "I believe God is one God who exists eternally as three distinct Persons, Father, Son, and Holy Spirit."

Bible receipts (pick 1–2): Matthew 3:16–17; Matthew 28:19

This changes my life because: "It means God has always been perfectly loving, and I am invited into that relationship."

One question I still have: (Write one honest question. No pretending.)

Short Prayer

Father, You are holy and perfectly good. Jesus, You are my Savior and my King. Holy Spirit, help me believe what is true when my mind gets confused. Thank You for being infinitely bigger than my ability to understand You. Amen.

My Notes & Thoughts

Brick #8: Providence: Is God Actually in Control?

Cold Open Moment

You've had this thought before. Usually, it happens late at night.

Maybe you are scrolling through the news, watching footage of a brutal war or a natural disaster that wiped out a town. Or maybe it hits much closer to home. You watch your parents get divorced, or your best friend gets diagnosed with a terrifying illness, and your brain immediately hits the emergency brakes.

Who is actually driving this bus?

If God is completely good and completely powerful, why does the world feel so violently out of control? It feels like we are in a car speeding down a mountain with no brakes, and God is just sitting in the passenger seat, hoping we don't crash.

When life shatters, you have a theological choice to make. You can believe that God is weak and couldn't stop the pain.

You can believe that God is cruel and caused the pain for fun. Or, you can discover the beautiful, heavy truth of what the Bible actually says about how God runs the universe.

Big Idea

God is not just a clockmaker who wound up the universe and walked away; He is actively directing every detail of history toward His perfect purpose.

Why This Matters

This doctrine is the ultimate cure for your deepest panic.

If God is not in control of the universe, then your life is determined by blind luck, random chance, and the terrible decisions of the people around you. That is a terrifying way to live.

But if God is actively sustaining and directing the world, it means your pain is never wasted. It means that even when you are walking through total darkness, the Author of the story has not dropped His pen. You aren't a victim of chaos; you are held by a King.

Key Words

- **Providence:** God's ongoing, continuous involvement in His creation, sustaining it and guiding it toward His goals.
- **Sovereignty:** God's absolute right and total power to rule over the entire universe.
- **Free Will:** The ability humans have to make real, meaningful choices for which they are held morally responsible.

Precision Note (grown-up wording): Theologians use the term *concurrence* to describe how God's sovereign direction and human free choices work together simultaneously without canceling each other out.

Bible Receipts

The Bible refuses to let us believe that the universe is running on autopilot.

The Apostle Paul is incredibly blunt about this when writing about Jesus. "He is before all things, and by him all things hold together" (Colossians 1:17, CSB). Gravity doesn't hold the universe together. The active, ongoing will of Jesus holds the universe together. If He stopped thinking about the world for a microsecond, we would all disintegrate.

But does God's control extend to the terrible things people do?

Look at the story of Joseph in the Old Testament. His brothers hated him, threw him in a pit, and sold him into slavery. Years later, Joseph is the second-in-command of Egypt and confronts his abusers. He says to them, "You planned evil against me; God planned it for good to bring about the present result, the survival of many people" (Genesis 50:20, CSB).

Notice what Joseph didn't say. He didn't say, "You did something evil, and God had to scramble to fix it." He said God was sovereignly planning good *through* their evil choices.

Truth in Plain English

God's providence means He is in the microscopic details of your life.

He didn't just create the Rocky Mountains and the oceans. Jesus explicitly said that not a single sparrow falls to the ground outside of the Father's care. He added, "Even the hairs of your head have all been counted" (Matthew 10:30, CSB).

Highlightable line: A God who numbers the hairs on your head is not a God who ignores the breaking of your heart.

God's providence does not mean bad things won't happen. We live in Act 2 (The Fall). But it does mean that bad things do not have the final say.

God is like a master chess player. He allows us to make our moves, even our rebellious, sinful moves, but He is so infinitely brilliant that He weaves our terrible choices into His ultimate victory.

Common Confusion Box

Confusion #1: "If God is in control of everything, then my choices don't matter." This sounds right because our human brains can't compute how God can be 100% in control while we are simultaneously 100% responsible for our actions (a concept called *fatalism*). But it's wrong. The Bible teaches both at the same time. You are not a robot; when you sin, it is your fault, not God's.

When you choose to pray, your prayers actually change things. God's sovereignty doesn't erase your choices; it gives your choices a framework to exist in.

Highlightable line: God's control isn't an excuse to be lazy; it is the confidence you need to be courageous.

Confusion #2: "If a tragedy happens, it means God caused evil to teach me a lesson." This sounds right because we desperately want to find a reason for our pain. But here is what Scripture shows instead: God never authors evil. James 1:13 says God cannot be tempted by evil, nor does He tempt anyone. God *allows* evil to exist for a time, and He can *use* the evil that humans commit to accomplish His good purposes (like the cross), but He is never the one pulling the trigger.

Why This Changes Real Life

When you actually believe in God's providence, you can finally exhale.

When you get rejected from the college you wanted to attend, or when you don't make the team, you don't have to spiral into a depression. You can grieve the disappointment, but you don't have to panic. Because if God closed that door, He is sovereignly guiding you to a different one.

You don't have to carry the weight of the world on your shoulders. You don't have to constantly obsess over making the "perfect" decision and ruining your life. You follow God's word the best you can, and you trust that His providence is big enough to catch you when you stumble.

Highlightable line: Peace isn't found by figuring out the future; peace is found by trusting the God who is already there.

Try This This Week

The "Rearview Mirror" exercise. Look back at a season in your life that was incredibly difficult, painful, or frustrating. Write down one way you can now clearly see God's fingerprints protecting you, changing you, or directing you through that specific pain.

Talk It Out

- When a situation in your life completely falls apart (like a rumor spreading or failing a major test), do you tend to blame God, blame yourself, or blame other people?
- Read Genesis 50:20 again. How does Joseph's view of his own trauma completely change the way we should view our enemies?
- Why is it actually comforting that God knows the number of hairs on your head?
- How does trusting in God's providence cure us from being "control freaks"?

BELIEF BUILDER (Brick #8: About God)

My one-sentence belief: "I believe God is completely sovereign, actively holding the universe together and directing all things for His good purposes."

Bible receipts (pick 1–2): Colossians 1:17; Genesis 50:20

This changes my life because: "I don't have to panic when life feels chaotic, because I know God is in the details."

One question I still have: (Write one honest question. No pretending.)

Short Prayer

Father, thank You that nothing in my life catches You by surprise. Jesus, thank You for holding the entire universe together with Your word. Holy Spirit, when my life feels like it is spinning out of control, anchor my mind to Your sovereignty. Forgive me for thinking I could run my life better than You. Help me to trust the Author of the story. Amen.

My Notes & Thoughts

PART 2 - CHECKPOINT

Assemble Your Second Statement Section: "About God"

You made it through Part 2. We covered some of the heaviest, most massive truths in the entire universe. Now, it's time to stop reading and start building the next section of your Statement of Faith.

At the end of the last five chapters, you wrote down five "bricks" (your one-sentence beliefs). In this checkpoint, you are going to edit those bricks and cement them together into a powerful paragraph explaining exactly who you believe God is.

Step 1: Gather Your Bricks

Look back at the Belief Builder sections from Chapters 4 through 8. Write your five one-sentence beliefs right here:

- **Brick 4 (Not a Bigger Human):** ______________________________
- **Brick 5 (Holy):** ______________________________
- **Brick 6 (Love):** ______________________________
- **Brick 7 (Trinity):** ______________________________
- **Brick 8 (Providence):** ______________________________

Step 2: Edit for Power

Look at the five sentences you just wrote. If you paste them all together right now, it will probably sound like a giant run-on sentence. You need to trim the fat.

Apply the **"Red Pen Rules"**:

1. **Combine the traits.** You don't need to start every sentence with "I believe God is..." You can combine them: "I believe God is the infinite Creator, perfectly holy, and fiercely loving."
2. **Make the Trinity clear.** Ensure your sentence about the Father, Son, and Holy Spirit is sharp and easy to understand.
3. **Upgrade your vocabulary.** Ensure you use strong theological words like *sovereign*, *holy*, or *Creator* instead of weak words like *big*, *good*, or *nice*.

Step 3: Draft Your Official Paragraph

Now, combine your edited bricks into one flowing paragraph. It should be 4–5 sentences maximum. This is the core of your theology. Make it strong.

My Statement of Faith: ABOUT GOD

(Example Draft: "I believe there is one God who exists eternally as three distinct Persons: Father, Son, and Holy Spirit. He is the infinite Creator of the universe and does not share my human limitations. God is perfectly holy and completely pure. He is the definition of love, fiercely committed to my ultimate good. He is completely sovereign, actively holding the universe together and directing all things according to His perfect purpose.")

Step 4: The 10-Second Spoken Test

Your Personal Statement of Faith has to survive the real world. If someone at the lunch table asks you, "So, what kind of God do you actually believe in?" you need a fast, anchored answer.

Look at your drafted paragraph and condense it into a single, spoken script that takes less than 10 seconds to say out loud.

My 10-Second Spoken Script:

"I believe in one God, Father, Son, and Holy Spirit, who is perfectly holy, fiercely loving, and completely in control of the universe."

Read your 10-second script out loud right now. Does it sound like something you would actually say? Keep tweaking the words until it feels authentic to your voice but perfectly true to the Bible.

Step 5: Log Your Receipts

Pick the **three strongest Bible verses** from Part 2 that back up your new paragraph, and write the references here so you always have the proof ready.

1. ________________________________ (Example: Matthew 3:16-17)
2. ________________________________ (Example: 1 John 4:8-10)
3. ________________________________ (Example: Colossians 1:17)

Congratulations. You have successfully defined the core of who God is. You are ready for Part 3.

<u>My Statement of Faith (after part 2)</u>

PART 3 - PEOPLE, PURPOSE, AND THE PROBLEM

In this part, we're talking about **you**, and what went wrong with the world. We'll unpack what it means to be made in God's image, why that gives you real dignity and purpose, and why sin is deeper than "breaking rules." We'll also face the hard stuff: brokenness, suffering, and the tension between God's justice and mercy. The goal is to help you write two key sections of your Statement of Faith: **what you believe about humanity and what you believe about sin**, in a way that makes sense of both your worth and your struggle.

Brick #9: Made in God's Image (Identity + Dignity)

Cold Open Moment

You know the routine. You take fourteen slightly different photos of yourself, analyze every single flaw, apply a filter, and finally post the best one.

Then, you wait. You watch the likes tick up, and for a few minutes, you feel a hit of validation. But an hour later, you see someone else's post, someone who is better looking, has better clothes, or just made varsity, and that validation evaporates.

You feel entirely average, crushed by the weight of comparing your everyday reality to everyone else's curated highlight reel.

We live in a world that constantly ranks human beings. We rank each other by GPA, by athletic ability, by follower count, and by physical appearance. And if you buy into that ranking system, you will spend your entire life exhausted, constantly trying to prove that you matter.

But what if your value was permanently fixed before you ever took your first breath? What if your identity wasn't an achievement you had to earn, but a completely unchangeable gift?

Big Idea

You are created in the image of God, which means your worth is absolute, permanent, and given to you by the Creator.

Why This Matters

Getting your identity right is a matter of spiritual survival.

If you build your identity on your grades, an injury can destroy you. If you build it on your relationships, a breakup will shatter you. But if your identity is rooted in the image of God, nothing can touch it.

- **It kills your insecurity.** You don't have to perform for a culture that will constantly change its mind about what is cool.
- **It changes how you treat others.** If every person has God's image, there is no such thing as an ordinary, worthless human being.

Key Words

- **Image of God:** The reality that humans are uniquely created to reflect God's character and rule on earth.
- **Dignity:** The inherent, unbreakable value that belongs to every single human being.
- **Identity:** Who you fundamentally are at your absolute core.
- **Soul:** The invisible, eternal part of you that makes you uniquely human and capable of knowing God.

Precision Note (grown-up wording): Theologians use the Latin phrase *Imago Dei* to describe the unique status of humanity as God's representatives on earth.

Bible Receipts

The very first chapter of the Bible drops a massive bomb on how we view human life.

After God creates the stars, the oceans, and the animals, He pauses. He does something entirely different for the grand finale. Genesis 1:27 (CSB) says, "So God created man in his own image; he created him in the image of God; he created them male and female."

You are not an evolved accident. You are a deliberate masterpiece.

King David understood the absolute wonder of this. When he was writing poetry to God about his own existence, he didn't focus on his accomplishments as king.

He wrote, "For it was you who created my inward parts; you knit me together in my mother's womb. I will praise you because I have been remarkably and wondrously made" (Psalm 139:13-14, CSB).

Before you could perform, speak, or achieve anything, God was intentionally knitting your life together with immense care.

Truth in Plain English

Being made in the image of God means you are a mirror.

You were designed to reflect God's love, creativity, justice, and kindness into the world. A stunning mountain range shows God's power, but a mountain cannot reflect the moral character of God. Only you can do that.

Highlightable line: Your value is not determined by what you do; your value is determined by Who made you.

This also means that every other person you look at is a mirror, too. The kid sitting alone in the cafeteria is made in the image of God. The politician you strongly disagree with is made in the image of God. The person who bullied you online is made in the image of God.

Because of this, racism is an attack on the image of God. Bullying is an attack on the image of God. Self-hatred is an attack on the image of God.

Common Confusion Box

Confusion #1: "If I fail, I lose my worth." This sounds right because society immediately cancels or discards people when they mess up. But it's wrong. The *Imago Dei* is not a trophy you win for good behavior. It is a birthright. Sin has deeply damaged the image of God inside of us, like a mirror that has been cracked, but it has not erased it. You cannot lose your inherent dignity, no matter how badly you fail.

Highlightable line: God doesn't love you because you are a good performer; He loves you because you are His creation.

Confusion #2: "My body doesn't matter, just my soul." This sounds right because we often hear people say "you are a soul that just happens to have a body." But here is what Scripture shows instead: God intentionally created your physical body, and He called it "very good." Christianity is not about escaping your physical body to float as a ghost. Your physical body matters to God, which means how you view your body, treat your body, and talk about your body matters deeply.

Why This Changes Real Life

When you actually believe you are made in the image of God, the relentless pressure to prove yourself evaporates.

You can walk into the cafeteria or scroll through your feed and stop viewing everyone as competition. You no longer have to tear someone else down just to make yourself feel taller. You can celebrate your friends' successes without feeling threatened by them.

It also drastically changes how you handle your own flaws. When you look in the mirror and hate what you see, you are arguing with the Artist who painted the canvas.

Resting in the *Imago Dei* means you can finally breathe. You can accept that you are flawed, while simultaneously knowing you are crowned with immense dignity and worth by the King of the universe.

Highlightable line: You don't have to hustle for your worth; you just have to rest in your Creator.

Try This This Week

The "Mirror Check." Sometime this week, while you are brushing your teeth and starting to criticize your appearance, look directly into the mirror and say out loud: 'I am remarkably and wondrously made.' It will feel incredibly awkward, but your brain needs to hear your own voice speak God's truth.

Talk It Out

- Why is it so incredibly easy to base our identity on our achievements (like grades or sports) instead of what God says about us?
- Read Genesis 1:27 again. How does the truth that both male and female are made in God's image impact how we should treat the opposite sex?
- Why is hating your own body or your own personality actually a theological issue, not just a psychological one?
- Think about someone at your school who is generally disliked. How does remembering they are made in the image of God change the way you view them?

BELIEF BUILDER (Brick #9: About People)

My one-sentence belief: "I believe every human being is remarkably made in the image of God and possesses absolute, permanent dignity."

Bible receipts (pick 1–2): Genesis 1:27; Psalm 139:13–14

This changes my life because: "I can stop ranking myself against others and trust that my worth is a gift from God."

One question I still have: (Write one honest question. No pretending.)

Short Prayer

Father, thank You for knitting me together with purpose and care. Jesus, thank You for restoring the image of God in me. Holy Spirit, when I feel worthless, remind me of my true identity. Help me to see the people around me the exact way You see them. Forgive me for the times I have treated Your creation with contempt. Amen.

My Notes & Thoughts

Brick #10: What Sin Really Is (not just mistakes)

Cold Open Moment

Listen to how people apologize today.

When someone gets caught doing something terrible, they usually post an apology online that goes something like this: "I made a mistake. I had a lapse in judgment. I wasn't acting like my true self."

We have completely sanitized the way we talk about our own darkness. We call our lies "white lies." We call our gossip "venting." We call our cruel outbursts "toxic traits" or say we just "woke up on the wrong side of the bed."

We desperately want to believe that deep down, we are fundamentally good people who just occasionally stumble into bad behavior. We want to believe that our issues are just surface-level scratches that can be buffed out with a little bit of self-improvement.

But if we lie about the disease, we will never seek the right cure. If you think your problem is just a lack of focus or bad habits, you only need a life coach and a better schedule. But if your problem is actual rebellion, you desperately need a Savior.

Big Idea

Sin isn't just a list of bad behaviors; it is a heart-level rebellion against God's good authority.

Why This Matters

This is the hardest truth to swallow, but it is the most necessary.

If you don don't understand the depth of sin, the cross of Jesus will look like a massive overreaction. You will look at Jesus bleeding on a piece of wood and think, *Did God really have to go to that extreme just because I cheated on a math test once?** **It kills self-righteousness.** When you realize what sin actually is, you stop looking down on other people.

- **It makes grace amazing.** You can't appreciate being rescued until you realize how hopelessly you were drowning.

Key Words

- **Sin:** Any failure to conform to the moral law of God in act, attitude, or nature.
- **Rebellion:** Deliberately choosing your own way over God's command.
- **Idolatry:** Loving, trusting, or prioritizing anything in the universe more than you love and trust God.
- **Depravity:** The reality that sin has infected every single part of human nature (our minds, our desires, our wills).

Precision Note (grown-up wording): Theologians use the term *Total Depravity*, which doesn't mean we are as evil as we could possibly be, but that sin has poisoned every aspect of our being, rendering us unable to save ourselves.

Bible Receipts

The Bible refuses to let us blame our sin on our circumstances or our friends.

Jesus was extremely blunt about where sin actually comes from. He said, "For from within, out of people's hearts, come evil thoughts, sexual immoralities, thefts, murders, adulteries, greed, evil actions, deceit, self-indulgence, envy, slander, pride, and foolishness. All these evil things come from within, and defile a person" (Mark 7:21-23, CSB).

Sin is an inside job. It doesn't happen to you; it comes *out* of you.

The Apostle Paul levels the playing field for the entire human race. He writes in Romans 3:23 (CSB), "For all have sinned and fall short of the glory of God." There are no VIPs. There are no "mostly good" people who get a pass.

And Paul doesn't mince words about the consequence of this rebellion. "For the wages of sin is death" (Romans 6:23, CSB). A wage is something you earn. When we declare independence from the God of life, the only paycheck we can possibly earn is death.

Truth in Plain English

Sin is cosmic treason.

It is looking directly at the Creator of the universe, the One who gave you air in your lungs, and saying, "Thanks for the life, but I know better than You. I want to be the boss."

Highlightable line: Sin isn't just breaking God's rules; it is an attempt to steal God's throne.

Every time you lie, every time you manipulate someone, every time you view someone with lust, you are committing idolatry. You are saying that your temporary pleasure is more valuable than God's eternal truth.

The scariest part about sin is that you don't even have to do anything outwardly bad to be guilty of it. You can be the nicest, most respectful kid in your youth group, volunteering every weekend, and still have a heart that is entirely full of pride, jealousy, and self-worship.

Common Confusion Box

Confusion #1: "I'm a good person compared to most people." This sounds right because we always grade on a curve. You think, *Well, I gossip sometimes, but at least I haven't killed anyone.* But it's wrong. God doesn't grade on a curve; He grades against His own perfect, blazing holiness. Compared to a serial killer, you look great. But compared to the absolute moral perfection of God, every single one of us falls infinitely short.

Highlightable line: Comparing your sin to someone else's sin is like bragging about drowning in 10 feet of water while they drown in 50 feet. You are both still drowning.

Confusion #2: "Sin is just God being strict about arbitrary rules." This sounds right because some church rules feel randomly made up just to stop people from having fun. But here is what Scripture shows instead: God's laws are not arbitrary. They are protective. God tells us not to lie, steal, or lust because those things destroy the joy and human flourishing He designed. Sin is God saying, "Do not drink poison," and us chugging it anyway just to prove nobody can tell us what to do.

Why This Changes Real Life

When you get painfully honest about your own sin, it completely changes how you exist in the world.

First, you stop being a hypocrite. When someone else messes up, your first instinct won't be to pull out your phone, judge them, and cancel them. Because you know the darkness of your own heart, your first instinct will be empathy.

Second, it stops the exhausting cycle of trying to hide your flaws. You don't have to pretend you have it all together. You can admit that you are deeply broken and in desperate need of help.

Highlightable line: You will never experience the freedom of God's grace until you admit the brutal reality of your own sin.

Owning your sin is the first step out of the darkness. It is terrifying for about ten seconds, and then it is the most liberating feeling in the world.

Try This This Week

The "No Excuses" Confession. Sometime this week, go to a quiet place and confess a specific sin to God out loud. Do not use the word "but." (Do not say, "I lied to my mom, *but* she was yelling at me.") Just own the treason. Say, "God, I did this. It was wrong. It was rebellion. Please forgive me."

Talk It Out

- Why do you think society works so hard to rename sin as "mistakes," "lapses," or "toxic traits"?
- Read Mark 7:21-23 again. Why is it actually more terrifying to know that sin comes from *inside* our hearts rather than outside pressure?
- Think of a rule God has given (like avoiding sexual immorality or not lying). How is that rule actually protecting you rather than just restricting you?
- How does realizing the depth of your own sin change the way you treat people who wrong you?

BELIEF BUILDER (Brick #10: About Sin)

My one-sentence belief: "I believe sin is a heart-level rebellion against God's authority that separates me from Him, and I am entirely guilty of it."

Bible receipts (pick 1–2): Mark 7:21–23; Romans 3:23

This changes my life because: "I can stop pretending I am perfect and humbly admit that I desperately need a Savior."

One question I still have: (Write one honest question. No pretending.)

Short Prayer

Father, I confess that I have rebelled against Your good authority. Jesus, thank You for not leaving me to drown in my own rebellion. Holy Spirit, give me the courage to stop making excuses for my sin. Expose the pride and idolatry hiding in my heart. Help me to run to Your grace instead of hiding in my shame. Amen.

My Notes & Thoughts

Brick #11: Why the World Is Broken (and why you feel it)

Cold Open Moment

You don't need a theology degree to know that something is deeply wrong with the world.

You feel it every time you open a news app and see headlines about another war, another school shooting, or another earthquake. You feel it when you sit at a funeral for someone who died way too young. You feel it late at night when a wave of anxiety hits your chest for absolutely no reason, making it hard to breathe.

There is an ache built into the human experience. It's a quiet, heavy grief that whispers: *Things are not supposed to be this way.* And you are absolutely right.

If you view the world without the Bible, this brokenness is just a meaningless tragedy. You just have to accept that life is a violent, random mess and then you die. But the Bible offers a radically different explanation for your pain. It validates your grief, and it gives you a reason for the ache.

Big Idea

The world is broken because human sin fractured creation, but your pain is proof that you were made for a better world.

Why This Matters

If you don't know why the world is broken, you will blame the wrong person.

You will either blame God, assuming He is cruel and enjoys watching us suffer, or you will blame yourself, assuming you are just too weak to handle life.

- **It validates your grief.** You aren't crazy for being upset when tragedy strikes; death is an intruder, not a friend.
- **It gives you perspective.** When you know the world is under a curse, you stop expecting it to give you perfect happiness.

Key Words

- **The Fall:** The historical moment when Adam and Eve rebelled, bringing sin and death into the world.
- **The Curse:** God's judgment on creation because of human sin, resulting in a world of decay, pain, and natural disasters.
- **Original Sin:** The corrupted, sinful nature that every human being inherits from Adam.

- **Groaning:** The deep, spiritual longing for God to fix what is broken and make the world new again.

Precision Note (grown-up wording): Theologians use the term *Federal Headship* to explain how Adam acted as the representative for all humanity; when he fell, the entire human race fell with him.

Bible Receipts

The Bible doesn't hide the brokenness of the world; it confronts it head-on.

In Genesis 3, when humanity first rebelled, God explained exactly what the consequences would be. It wasn't just a slap on the wrist. God told Adam that the very ground was cursed because of him. "It will produce thorns and thistles for you... You will eat bread by the sweat of your brow until you return to the ground" (Genesis 3:18-19, CSB).

Sin didn't just break the human heart. It broke the soil. It broke the weather. It broke our biology.

The Apostle Paul explains how creation is reacting to this curse right now. "For we know that the whole creation has been groaning together with labor pains until now. Not only that, but we ourselves who have the Spirit groan inwardly as we eagerly wait for adoption, the redemption of our bodies" (Romans 8:22-23, CSB).

Labor pains. The earthquakes, the diseases, and the deep anxiety in your chest, that is the sound of a universe groaning under the weight of sin, waiting to be rescued.

Truth in Plain English

Imagine a kid taking a baseball bat to a massive, beautiful mirror.

When Adam and Eve sinned, they swung the bat. The mirror shattered into a billion pieces. God's perfect creation was fractured.

This is why we have cancer. This is why we have betrayals, car accidents, and depression. It is all collateral damage from the Fall. God didn't create a world with childhood leukemia or school bullies; humans invited the curse of death into the living room, and now we are living in the wreckage.

Highlightable line: You feel like you don't belong in a world of death and pain because you were originally designed for a world of life and peace.

Your frustration with the world is actually a deeply theological emotion. When you get furiously angry at injustice, or when you weep over a casket, you are echoing the heart of God. You are agreeing with the Creator that *this is not how the story was supposed to go.*

Common Confusion Box

Confusion #1: "If God is good, He would just wipe out all the evil in the world." This sounds right because a good judge should stop criminals. We want God to show up tonight and eradicate every trace of evil on the planet. But it's wrong because if God wiped out all evil tonight at midnight, none of us would be here at 12:01. We are part of the problem. God is holding back His final judgment right now out of extreme patience, giving rebellious humans time to repent and be saved.

Highlightable line: God hasn't forgotten the brokenness of the world; He is just delaying the end of the story so more people can be saved.

Confusion #2: "If we just get better politicians or more technology, we can fix the world." This sounds right because humans have made incredible advancements in medicine and science. But here is what Scripture shows instead: You cannot cure a spiritual curse with a technological bandage. We can make life more comfortable, but we cannot defeat death, and we cannot force the human heart to stop being selfish. Only the return of Jesus can permanently fix the world.

Why This Changes Real Life

Understanding the Fall takes a massive amount of pressure off your shoulders.

First, it allows you to stop expecting a perfect life. You don't have to be shocked or completely disillusioned when a friend betrays you, or when you get sick, or when a plan fails. You live in a fractured world. Acknowledging the brokenness helps you survive it without losing your faith.

Second, it turns you into a person of deep empathy. When you see someone crying in the hallway, or when you watch someone struggling with severe anxiety, you don't judge them. You know they are just feeling the sharp edges of the shattered mirror.

You get to sit with them in the dark, acknowledge that the world is broken, and remind them that the King is coming back to put the pieces together.

Try This This Week

The "Groan and Hope" prayer. When you see something terrible happen this week (on the news, at school, or in your own life), pause for ten seconds. Pray: *"God, this is broken and it hurts. Please come back and fix it."* You are aligning your heart with the groaning of creation.

Talk It Out

- When was a specific moment you realized, "Things are not supposed to be this way"?
- Read Romans 8:22-23 again. How does the metaphor of "labor pains" change the way we view the suffering in the world?
- Why is it actually a relief to know that the brokenness in the world is the result of the Fall, rather than just God being cruel?
- How should Christians react to tragedies in the world differently than people who don't know the Bible?

BELIEF BUILDER (Brick #11: About Sin)

My one-sentence belief: "I believe human sin fractured God's perfect creation, bringing death, pain, and brokenness into the entire world."

Bible receipts (pick 1–2): Genesis 3:18–19; Romans 8:22–23

This changes my life because: "It gives me a reason for the pain I feel and allows me to stop expecting a perfect life in a fallen world."

One question I still have: (Write one honest question. No pretending.)

Short Prayer

Father, my heart aches when I see the pain and injustice in the world. Jesus, thank You for stepping into our brokenness instead of staying far away. Holy Spirit, comfort me when the weight of the Fall feels too heavy to carry. Give me deep empathy for the hurting people around me. I am eagerly waiting for You to make all things new. Amen.

My Notes & Thoughts

Brick #12: Justice and Mercy (how both can be true)

Cold Open Moment

We all love justice when we are the victims.

If someone steals your phone, wrecks your car, or spreads a vicious rumor about you, you want them held accountable. You want them to pay. You want the principal, the police, or the universe to step in and deliver absolute, unrelenting justice.

But when the roles are reversed, when *you* are the one who lied, when *you* are the one who cheated, when *you* are the one who hurt someone else, suddenly, you don't want justice at all. You want a second chance. You want understanding. You want mercy.

We want a God who crushes our enemies with strict justice, but treats us with soft mercy.

But God cannot be bribed, and God does not play favorites. He is infinitely just, which means every single sin must be punished. And He is infinitely merciful, which means He desperately wants to forgive you.

So how does God punish the sin without destroying the sinner?

Big Idea

God is perfectly just and must punish sin, but He is perfectly merciful and took that punishment on Himself.

Why This Matters

This is the absolute core of the Christian faith. If you don't understand how God's justice and mercy work together, the cross of Jesus makes absolutely zero sense.

- **It proves God is good.** A judge who lets murderers go free isn't loving; he's corrupt. God's justice means evil actually gets defeated.
- **It secures your freedom.** You don't have to wonder if God will change His mind and punish you later, because the bill has already been paid.

Key Words

- **Justice:** God doing what is exactly right, ensuring that all sin gets the precise punishment it deserves.
- **Mercy:** God choosing to withhold the terrible punishment that we rightfully earned.
- **Wrath:** God's perfect, holy, and settled anger against all evil and injustice.

- **Substitution:** Someone stepping in to take the punishment on behalf of someone else.

Precision Note (grown-up wording): The theological term for Jesus taking our punishment is *Penal Substitutionary Atonement*, He took our penalty (penal) in our place (substitution) to make us right with God (atonement).

Bible Receipts

The Apostle Paul wrote a paragraph in the book of Romans that might be the most important theological statement ever written.

He explains exactly how God solved the problem of human sin. "God presented him [Jesus] as an atoning sacrifice in his blood, received through faith, to demonstrate his righteousness, because in his restraint God passed over the sins previously committed" (Romans 3:25, CSB).

Paul is saying that for centuries, God had been mercifully holding back His full wrath against human sin. But a good judge can't ignore crimes forever. Justice had to be served.

So what did God do? Paul drops the hammer in the next verse: "...to demonstrate his righteousness at the present time, so that he would be just and justify the one who has faith in Jesus" (Romans 3:26, CSB).

Just and the justifier. God executes perfect justice (by punishing sin on the cross) so that He can be the one who justifies us (giving us mercy).

The Apostle Paul later writes to the Ephesians, "But God, who is rich in mercy, because of his great love that he had for us, made us alive with Christ even though we were dead in trespasses" (Ephesians 2:4-5, CSB).

Truth in Plain English

Imagine you are standing in a courtroom. You are guilty. You have committed high treason, and the judge sentences you to a massive, unpayable fine.

If the judge just says, "You know what, don't worry about it, you're free to go," that judge is corrupt. The law demands a penalty.

But imagine the judge bangs the gavel, declares you fully guilty, and sets the fine. Then, the judge takes off his robe, steps down from the bench, pulls out his own wallet, and pays the fine for you.

The law is satisfied. Justice is served. But you get to walk free.

Highlightable line: At the cross of Jesus, the perfect justice of God and the perfect mercy of God violently collided.

God didn't sweep your sin under the rug. He didn't just ignore it. He took the blazing heat of His own holy justice against your sin and absorbed it into His own body on the cross. Jesus drank the cup of God's wrath so that you could drink the cup of His mercy.

Common Confusion Box

Confusion #1: "The Old Testament God is angry and just, but New Testament Jesus is nice and merciful." This sounds right because people love to separate God the Father from Jesus, acting like Jesus had to step in to protect us from an abusive Father. But it's wrong. God the Father and God the Son planned this rescue mission together in perfect harmony. John 3:16 says, "For God loved the world in this way: He gave his one and only Son." The cross wasn't Jesus protecting us from the Father; it was the Father giving up His Son to save us.

Highlightable line: Jesus didn't die to change God's mind about you; Jesus died because God had already made up His mind to save you.

Confusion #2: "If God is merciful, why does hell exist?" This sounds right because hell is a terrifying reality, and it seems contradictory to a God of love. But here is what Scripture shows instead: Hell exists precisely because God is just. He will not force rebels who have hated Him for a lifetime to spend eternity in His presence. Hell is the terrifying reality of God handing people over to the absolute freedom they demanded, existence without Him.

Why This Changes Real Life

When you grasp the cross, where justice and mercy meet, it shatters your pride and kills your shame.

It kills your pride because you realize you didn't earn your salvation. You were guilty in the courtroom. You cannot look down on anyone else, because you are only breathing today because of someone else's blood.

And it kills your shame. When you mess up on a Friday night, the enemy will whisper in your ear, "God is disgusted with you. He is going to make you pay for that."

You can look right back and say, "No. God is perfectly just, which means He will never demand two payments for the same sin. Jesus already paid for this."

You are fully known, fully exposed, and fully forgiven.

Try This This Week

The "Paid in Full" reminder. Take a red pen and write the word *PAID* on a small piece of paper. Put it inside your phone case or your wallet. Every time you feel crushed by guilt over a past mistake, look at that word and remember that God's justice is already completely satisfied.

Talk It Out

- Why do we naturally want strict justice for other people but unlimited mercy for ourselves?
- Read Romans 3:26 again. Why is it so important that God is both the "just" AND the "justifier"? What happens if He is only one of those things?
- How does the cross prove that God takes sin seriously?
- Think about the "courtroom" analogy. How does knowing your fine has been paid by the Judge change the way you live your life?

BELIEF BUILDER (Brick #12: About Sin/Salvation)

My one-sentence belief: "I believe God is perfectly just to punish sin, but perfectly merciful to take that punishment upon Himself through Jesus."

Bible receipts (pick 1–2): Romans 3:25–26; Ephesians 2:4–5

This changes my life because: "I don't have to carry the crushing weight of my own guilt, because justice was fully served at the cross."

One question I still have: (Write one honest question. No pretending.)

Short Prayer

Father, thank You that You are a perfectly just Judge who does not ignore evil. Jesus, thank You for stepping down from the bench to pay the fine I owed. Holy Spirit, remind me of the cross when I feel overwhelmed by shame. Keep me from taking Your mercy for granted. Help me to show the same mercy to others that You have shown to me. Amen.

My Notes & Thoughts

PART 3 - CHECKPOINT

Assemble Your Third Statement Section: "About People & Sin"

You made it through Part 3. You just tackled the highest highs of human dignity and the lowest lows of human rebellion. Now it's time to stop reading and start building the next section of your Statement of Faith.

At the end of the last four chapters, you wrote down four "bricks" (your one-sentence beliefs). Because this section covers two massive topics, you are going to draft *two* short paragraphs in this checkpoint.

Step 1: Gather Your Bricks

Look back at the Belief Builder sections from Chapters 9 through 12. Write your four one-sentence beliefs right here:

- **Brick 9 (Image of God):** ________________________________
- **Brick 10 (What Sin Is):** ________________________________
- **Brick 11 (The Broken World):** ________________________________
- **Brick 12 (Justice and Mercy):** ________________________________

Step 2: Edit for Power

Look at the sentences you just wrote. Apply the **"Red Pen Rules"**:

1. **Group them logically.** Bricks 9 and 11 will form your paragraph on "About People." Bricks 10 and 12 will form your paragraph on "About Sin."
2. **Cut the apologies.** Remove any weak phrases. Don't say "I feel like sin is bad." Say "Sin is rebellion."
3. **Upgrade your vocabulary.** Ensure you use strong theological words like *dignity*, *Imago Dei*, *rebellion*, and *justice*.

Step 3: Draft Your Official Paragraphs

Now, write out your two flowing paragraphs. Keep them punchy and clear.

My Statement of Faith: ABOUT PEOPLE

(Example Draft: "I believe every human being is remarkably made in the image of God and possesses absolute, permanent dignity. We were designed to reflect God's character. However, because of human sin, we live in a fractured, fallen world that is filled with death, pain, and brokenness.")

My Statement of Faith: ABOUT SIN

(Example Draft: "I believe sin is not just a mistake, but a heart-level rebellion against God's authority that infects every part of human nature. Because God is perfectly just, He must punish sin. But because He is perfectly merciful, He chose to take that punishment upon Himself through Jesus.")

Step 4: The 10-Second Spoken Test

If a friend at school asks you, "Why do Christians think everyone is so bad?" you need a fast, anchored answer that balances our dignity with our brokenness.

Look at your drafted paragraphs and condense them into a single, spoken script.

My 10-Second Spoken Script:

"I believe humans have incredible dignity because God made us, but our hearts are deeply broken by our rebellion against Him."

Read your 10-second script out loud right now. Practice it until it feels completely natural to say.

Step 5: Log Your Receipts

Pick the **three strongest Bible verses** from Part 3 that back up your new paragraphs, and write the references here.

1. ______________________ (Example: Genesis 1:27)
2. ______________________ (Example: Romans 3:23)
3. ______________________ (Example: Romans 3:25-26)

Congratulations. You have successfully defined the reality of the human condition. You are ready for Part 4.

My Statement of Faith (after part 3)

PART 4 - JESUS: THE CENTER

In this part, everything narrows to Jesus, because Christianity isn't mainly a set of morals, it's a Person. We'll explore who Jesus is (fully God and fully man), what He came to do, and why the cross and resurrection aren't just religious symbols, they're the heart of hope. The goal is to help you build a strong "About Jesus" section for your Statement of Faith that's clear, Bible-grounded, and personal, so if someone asks, "Why Jesus?" you don't freeze. You'll have words.

Brick #13: Jesus Fully God and Fully Man

Cold Open Moment

Think about how superheroes work in the movies.

Usually, the hero has a secret identity. Clark Kent takes off his glasses, unbuttons his shirt, and suddenly he is Superman. The clumsy reporter act was just a costume he wore to blend in with normal people.

When a lot of people think about Jesus, they secretly imagine Him like Superman. They think He was fully God, but just walking around in a human "costume" for thirty-three years. They assume that when Jesus got tired, He was just faking it to fit in. They assume that when He cried, it was just acting.

But if Jesus was just faking His humanity, then He cannot actually relate to your pain. And if He wasn't fully human, He couldn't actually step into your place to take your punishment.

Jesus didn't just put on a human costume. He actually became one of us.

Big Idea

Jesus is one hundred percent God and one hundred percent human, all at the same time, without either nature canceling the other out.

Why This Matters

This isn't just a brain-teaser; it is the linchpin of your salvation.

If Jesus was only human, His death on the cross would only be a tragedy. A mere human cannot pay the infinite debt of sin for the entire world. But if Jesus was only God, He couldn't die at all, and He couldn't serve as a substitute for humanity.

- **He is the perfect bridge.** Because He is God, He can reach the Father; because He is human, He can reach us.
- **He actually understands.** When you pray to Jesus about your exhaustion or your heartbreak, He doesn't just sympathize from a distance; He knows exactly what it feels like.

Key Words

- **Incarnation:** The moment God the Son stepped out of eternity and took on a physical, human nature.
- **Divine Nature:** All the attributes that make God who He is (infinite, all-powerful, holy).
- **Human Nature:** The reality of having a physical body, a human mind, and human emotions (but without sin).

- **Substitute:** Someone who takes the place of another person to absorb their penalty.

Precision Note (grown-up wording): Theologians call this the *Hypostatic Union*, meaning Jesus is one Person who holds two distinct natures (divine and human) perfectly united forever.

Bible Receipts

The Bible doesn't try to hide this tension; it puts it front and center.

Look at how the Apostle John starts his Gospel. He writes, "In the beginning was the Word, and the Word was with God, and the Word was God" (John 1:1, CSB). This establishes that Jesus (the Word) is completely, eternally God.

But just a few verses later, John drops the biggest plot twist in human history. "The Word became flesh and dwelt among us. We observed his glory, the glory as the one and only Son from the Father, full of grace and truth" (John 1:14, CSB).

The Creator of the stars became a microscopic embryo.

The Apostle Paul explains the attitude Jesus had about this in Philippians 2:6-7 (CSB). He writes that Jesus, "existing in the form of God, did not consider equality with God as something to be exploited. Instead he emptied himself by assuming the form of a servant, taking on the likeness of humanity."

Jesus didn't empty Himself of His "God-ness." He emptied Himself of His *privileges*, choosing to experience the brutal reality of human life.

Truth in Plain English

To understand Jesus, you have to hold two massive truths in your hands at the exact same time.

First, hold His humanity. Jesus got incredibly tired and slept in the back of a boat. He was thirsty and asked for water. He wept openly at the grave of His friend. He was tempted. His muscles ached, and His physical body died.

Second, hold His deity. That exact same Jesus woke up from His nap and told a hurricane to shut up, and it obeyed. He turned water into wine. He forgave sins, something only God has the authority to do. And He physically walked out of His own tomb.

Highlightable line: Jesus wasn't half-God and half-man; He was completely God and completely man.

He didn't mix the two natures together like a smoothie. His divine nature didn't dilute His human pain, and His human nature didn't diminish His divine power. He is the infinite God experiencing life from the inside of a fragile human body.

Common Confusion Box

Confusion #1: "Jesus gave up His divine powers to become human." This sounds right because it is hard to imagine God limiting Himself to a human body. But it's wrong. If Jesus gave up His divinity, He would cease to be God, which is impossible. He didn't lose His power; He just voluntarily restricted how He used it. He lived His earthly life in complete submission to the Father and in the power of the Holy Spirit, perfectly modeling how humans were originally designed to live.

Highlightable line: The incarnation wasn't God subtracting His power; it was God adding a human nature to Himself.

Confusion #2: "Jesus is like Hercules, a demigod who is part human and part divine." This sounds right if you grew up watching Greek mythology movies. But here is what Scripture shows instead: A demigod is a mutant. A demigod isn't fully divine, and he isn't fully human. Jesus isn't a 50/50 split. He is 100% God and 100% human.

Why This Changes Real Life

Knowing that Jesus is fully human completely changes the way you talk to Him.

When you go through a season of intense anxiety, you don't have to pray to a distant God who has no idea what a panic attack feels like. On the night before He died, Jesus was in such deep psychological distress that He sweat drops of blood.

When your friends betray you, you don't have to explain the sting of rejection to Him. Jesus had His closest friend sell Him out for a bag of coins.

Highlightable line: Because Jesus became human, there is absolutely no pain in your life that He cannot understand from personal experience.

He isn't just a King sitting safely on a throne giving you advice. He is a King who stepped down into the mud, fought your battles, took your wounds, and paved the way home.

Try This This Week

The "He Gets It" Prayer. The next time you feel a very human emotion this week (exhaustion, sadness, or frustration), start your prayer by acknowledging His humanity. Say: *"Jesus, You know exactly what it feels like to be this exhausted. Help me right now."* ### Talk It Out

- Why do you think it is so common for people to pretend Jesus wasn't fully human (like assuming He didn't actually feel pain)?
- Read John 1:1 and 1:14 again. How does knowing that the Creator of the universe became a human completely change how you view God's love for us?
- Which is harder for you to wrap your mind around: the fact that Jesus is fully God, or the fact that Jesus is fully man?
- How does knowing Jesus experienced temptation, betrayal, and deep sadness change the way you pray to Him?

BELIEF BUILDER (Brick #13: About Jesus)

My one-sentence belief: "I believe Jesus Christ is the Son of God, fully divine and fully human, making Him the only perfect bridge between God and humanity."

Bible receipts (pick 1–2): John 1:1, 14; Philippians 2:6–7

This changes my life because: "I can trust Jesus with my deepest pain, knowing He has experienced the reality of human suffering firsthand."

One question I still have: (Write one honest question. No pretending.)

Short Prayer

Father, thank You for sending Your Son to rescue a broken world. Jesus, thank You for not staying far away in heaven, but stepping into our mess. Holy Spirit, help me to grasp the absolute miracle of the incarnation. When I feel isolated, remind me that I follow a Savior who understands my tears. Amen.

My Notes & Thoughts

Brick #14: Why Jesus Came (King + Savior)

Cold Open Moment

Have you ever met someone famous, or maybe just someone you followed online, and realized they were absolutely nothing like you expected?

Maybe their personality was totally different, or they were way shorter in person. When the image in your head clashes with the reality standing in front of you, it creates a massive sense of whiplash.

This is exactly what happened when Jesus showed up on earth.

The people of Israel had been waiting centuries for a Messiah. They had built up a very specific profile in their minds. They expected a ruthless military general who would ride into Jerusalem on a warhorse, slaughter the Roman army, fix the economy, and make their lives completely comfortable.

Instead, they got a carpenter from a nowhere town who rode a donkey, hung out with tax collectors, and washed His followers' dirty feet. He didn't fit their mold. But Jesus didn't come to meet their expectations; He came to actually save them.

Big Idea

Jesus didn't just come to be a good teacher; He came to rescue us as a Savior and rule the world as its true King.

Why This Matters

If you misunderstand why Jesus came, you will constantly be disappointed with Him.

If you think Jesus came just to make you happy, you will walk away from your faith the moment you get depressed. If you think He came just to give you good advice, you will only listen to Him when it is convenient.

- **He is a Savior.** This means you don't have to save yourself, clean yourself up, or fix your own heart.
- **He is a King.** This means He has the absolute authority to tell you how to live your life.

Key Words

- **Savior:** Someone who rescues you from a fatal danger that you cannot escape on your own.
- **Lord (King):** Someone who has absolute authority and the right to demand your total allegiance.
- **Kingdom of God:** The reign and rule of God breaking into the broken world through Jesus.
- **Messiah:** The Hebrew word for "Anointed One" (Christ in Greek), the long-awaited King who would save God's people.

Precision Note (grown-up wording): Theologians talk about the Kingdom of God as being *already but not yet*, Jesus has already inaugurated His Kingdom, but it will not be fully realized until He returns.

Bible Receipts

Jesus was very clear about His own mission statement.

At the very beginning of His ministry, He walked into the region of Galilee and announced exactly what He was doing. "The time is fulfilled, and the kingdom of God has come near. Repent and believe the good news!" (Mark 1:15, CSB).

He didn't announce a new religion or a new set of rules. He announced a Kingdom. And a Kingdom means there is a King who is taking His territory back from the darkness.

But this King operated completely differently than human politicians. He explained His strategy in Luke 19:10 (CSB): "For the Son of Man has come to seek and to save the lost."

He didn't come to recruit the rich, the powerful, and the perfect. He came specifically to find the people who were completely wrecked by sin, broken by shame, and entirely lost. He came to save them.

Truth in Plain English

You cannot split Jesus in half.

Many people today want Jesus to be their Savior, but they absolutely do not want Him to be their King. They want Him to forgive their sins, punch their ticket to heaven, and comfort them when they are sad. But they want to remain the boss of their own lives. They want to dictate their own schedules, their own dating lives, and their own money.

Highlightable line: You cannot hire Jesus as your Savior and fire Him as your King.

If He is God, He gets the throne. He gets the final say over how you treat your enemies, how you use your phone, and how you view the world.

At the same time, some people view Jesus *only* as a King. They view Him as a strict boss who is constantly judging their performance. They forget that this King loved His subjects so fiercely that He took off His crown, stepped off His throne, and died to pay their debts.

Common Confusion Box

Confusion #1: "Jesus was just a great moral teacher who wanted us to be nice to each other." This sounds right because Jesus did teach incredible things, like loving our enemies and caring for the poor. But it's wrong because it ignores His wildest claims. A "good teacher" doesn't claim to have the authority to forgive sins. A "good teacher" doesn't claim that He will personally judge the world at the end of time. As C.S. Lewis famously pointed out, a man who claims to be God is either a lunatic, a liar, or the Lord. "Just a good teacher" is not an option.

Highlightable line: Jesus didn't come to give bad people good advice; He came to give dead people new life.

Confusion #2: "If Jesus is King, why is the world still so messed up?" This sounds right because we expect a victorious King to immediately fix all the problems in His territory. But here is what Scripture shows instead: Jesus conquered sin and death at the cross (the Kingdom is *already* here), but He has not yet returned to execute final judgment and remove all evil (the Kingdom is *not yet* fully complete). We live in the middle space.

Why This Changes Real Life

Submitting to Jesus as King feels terrifying at first, but it is actually the most liberating thing you can do.

Right now, you are probably acting as the king of your own life. And if you are honest, the crown is way too heavy for you. The pressure to manage your own reputation, secure your own future, and figure out your own truth is exhausting.

When you bow to Jesus as King, you get to take the crown off.

You don't have to carry the weight of the world anymore. You get to follow His rules, knowing that His rules are designed by a King who already proved He is willing to die for you. You can trust His authority because you have seen His love.

Highlightable line: Surrendering to Jesus doesn't ruin your freedom; it rescues you from the exhausting job of being your own boss.

Try This This Week

The "Your Kingdom Come" Audit. Grab a piece of paper and write down three major areas of your life (e.g., My Phone, My Friendships, My Future Plans). Next to each one, honestly write who is currently acting as the "King" of that area, you or Jesus.

Talk It Out

- Why were the people of Israel so disappointed when Jesus didn't show up as a military conqueror?
- Why is it so tempting to want Jesus as a Savior (to forgive us) but reject Him as a King (to lead us)?
- Read Luke 19:10 again. How does Jesus' mission to "seek and save the lost" change the way you view people who are currently making terrible life choices?
- What is one specific area of your life where it is really hard to let Jesus be the King?

BELIEF BUILDER (Brick #14: About Jesus)

My one-sentence belief: "I believe Jesus came not just to be a moral teacher, but to rescue me as my Savior and rule my life as my King."

Bible receipts (pick 1–2): Mark 1:15; Luke 19:10

This changes my life because: "I can step down from trying to be the boss of my own life and trust His perfect leadership."

One question I still have: (Write one honest question. No pretending.)

Short Prayer

Father, thank You for sending the exact King we needed, not the one we expected. Jesus, forgive me for the times I have wanted Your forgiveness but rejected Your authority. Holy Spirit, help me to joyfully surrender every area of my life to the Kingdom of God. Take the heavy crown off my head. I want You to be the boss. Amen.

My Notes & Thoughts

Brick #15: The Cross: What Happened There

Cold Open Moment

We have entirely sanitized the cross.

We wear crosses as silver necklaces. We get them tattooed on our forearms. We print them on cool T-shirts with trendy fonts. We are so used to seeing the shape of the cross that we have completely forgotten what it actually was.

In the ancient world, the cross wasn't jewelry. It was a weapon of terror. It was the Roman Empire's most brutal, humiliating form of torture and execution. If you wore a necklace of a cross in the first century, it would be the modern equivalent of wearing a necklace shaped like an electric chair or a lethal injection needle.

It was a symbol of absolute defeat, pain, and shame.

So how did the worst instrument of death in human history become the ultimate symbol of hope and love? To understand that, you have to understand what was actually happening when Jesus was hanging on that wood. He wasn't just dying. He was doing business.

Big Idea

On the cross, Jesus acted as our perfect substitute, absorbing the holy wrath of God against our sin so we could receive His grace.

Why This Matters

If you don't understand what happened at the cross, your faith will always rely on your own performance.

You will constantly wonder if you are "good enough" for God. You will wonder if your sins are actually forgiven, or if God is secretly keeping a scorecard. But when you understand the mechanics of the cross, the guessing games stop.

- **It proves it is finished.** You cannot add to the payment Jesus made.
- **It destroys your shame.** Your worst, darkest sins have already been punished, meaning God will never bring them up to shame you again.

Key Words

- **Atonement:** The act of making things right between God and humanity by paying the penalty for sin.
- **Justification:** God legally declaring you "not guilty" and perfectly righteous, not because you are perfect, but because Jesus' perfect record is given to you.
- **Wrath:** God's perfect, holy, and settled anger against all evil and injustice.
- **Grace:** God giving you an incredible gift (salvation) that you absolutely did not earn and do not deserve.

Precision Note (grown-up wording): Theologians talk about the *Great Exchange* (or imputation), our sin was placed onto Jesus, and His perfect righteousness was placed onto us.

Bible Receipts

The Apostle Paul gives us the clearest, most staggering explanation of the cross in the entire New Testament.

He writes, "He made the one who did not know sin to be sin for us, so that in him we might become the righteousness of God" (2 Corinthians 5:21, CSB).

Read that again. It is the ultimate transaction. Jesus had no sin; He had a perfect record. You have a massive record of sin and rebellion. On the cross, God took your filthy, broken record and handed it to Jesus. Then, He took Jesus' flawless, perfect record and handed it to you.

Hundreds of years before Jesus was even born, the prophet Isaiah predicted exactly how this would work.

"But he was pierced because of our rebellion, crushed because of our iniquities; punishment for our peace was on him, and we are healed by his wounds" (Isaiah 53:5, CSB).

Jesus wasn't killed just because the Roman government hated Him. He was crushed because justice demanded it, and He voluntarily stepped into the path of that justice for us.

Truth in Plain English

Think about the cross like a massive courtroom.

You are the defendant, and you are guilty of cosmic treason. The Judge (God) is perfectly holy. The penalty for treason is death. But Jesus steps into the courtroom, stands next to you, and says, "I will take the sentence."

When Jesus was hanging in the darkness on Friday afternoon, He wasn't just experiencing physical pain. The full, terrifying weight of God's holy wrath against every lie, every murder, every act of racism, and every ounce of human pride was poured out onto Jesus.

Highlightable line: On the cross, Jesus was treated the way you deserve to be treated, so that you could be treated the way He deserves to be treated.

When Jesus yelled, "It is finished!" right before He died, He meant it. The debt was fully paid. The wrath was exhausted. There is not a single drop of punishment left for anyone who puts their trust in Him.

Common Confusion Box

Confusion #1: "The cross was basically cosmic child abuse; God the Father forced Jesus to suffer." This sounds right to critics who don't understand the Trinity. They imagine an angry Father taking His rage out on an innocent, unwilling Son. But it's wrong. The Father and the Son are one. Jesus said clearly in John 10:18, "No one takes my life from me, but I lay it down on my own." The cross was a rescue mission planned in perfect unity by the Trinity.

Highlightable line: The cross wasn't an accident, a tragedy, or a failure; it was the most brilliant rescue mission in the history of the universe.

Confusion #2: "Jesus died just to show us a good example of how to love people." This sounds right because the cross *is* the ultimate example of love and sacrifice. But here is what Scripture shows instead: If a man jumps in front of a train to save a child pushed onto the tracks, that is a heroic rescue. But if a man just randomly jumps in front of a train and says, "Look how much I love you!" that isn't a rescue; it's insane. Jesus didn't just die to show off His love. He died because the train of God's holy justice was coming straight for us, and He threw Himself on the tracks.

Why This Changes Real Life

Understanding the Great Exchange is the only way to silence the accusing voices in your head.

When you fail a massive test of character, when you lie to your parents, betray a friend, or fall back into a destructive habit, the enemy will immediately tell you that you are worthless. He will tell you that God is finally fed up with you.

But if you understand the cross, you can fight back.

You can look at your own failure and say, "Yes, I am a mess. Yes, I deserve judgment. But my judgment already happened on a hill outside Jerusalem 2,000 years ago. God is perfectly just, and He will not demand two payments for the same sin."

Highlightable line: Because of the cross, God doesn't just tolerate you; when He looks at you, He sees the perfect record of His Son.

You are completely free. You don't have to perform to earn God's love, and you don't have to hide in shame when you mess up.

Try This This Week

The "Great Exchange" Visual. Take a sticky note and draw a simple cross. On the left side, write one specific sin or failure you constantly feel guilty about. On the right side, write the word *RIGHTEOUS*. Draw an arrow from your sin to the cross, and an arrow from the cross to the word *RIGHTEOUS*. Throw away your guilt.

Talk It Out

- Why do you think modern culture likes the image of the cross as a piece of jewelry, but hates talking about the reality of God's wrath?
- Read 2 Corinthians 5:21 again. Try to explain "The Great Exchange" in your own words.
- How does knowing that Jesus *volunteered* for the cross change the way you view His love for you?
- If God has already legally declared you "not guilty," why is it so hard for us to forgive ourselves when we mess up?

BELIEF BUILDER (Brick #15: About Jesus)

My one-sentence belief: "I believe Jesus died on the cross as my perfect substitute, taking the punishment for my sin so I could receive His perfect righteousness."

Bible receipts (pick 1–2): 2 Corinthians 5:21; Isaiah 53:5

This changes my life because: "I don't have to live in fear of God's anger, because my debt has been completely paid."

One question I still have: (Write one honest question. No pretending.)

Short Prayer

Father, thank You for the brilliant, terrifying, beautiful plan of the cross. Jesus, I can never repay You for taking the wrath that I deserved. Holy Spirit, when I am drowning in shame over my own sin, anchor my heart to the Great Exchange. Help me to stop trying to earn what You have already given me for free. Amen.

My Notes & Thoughts

Brick #16: The Resurrection: Why It Changes Everything

Cold Open Moment

Think about how history classes work.

When you study a famous historical figure, like Abraham Lincoln, Martin Luther King Jr., or Julius Caesar, the story always ends the exact same way. They did incredible things, they changed the world, and then they died. If you want to honor them today, you go visit their graves.

For the first three days after Jesus died, His followers thought they were living in that exact same kind of story. Jesus had been a brilliant teacher and a powerful leader, but the Roman government executed Him. The story was over. They were hiding in a locked room, completely terrified, waiting to see if they were going to be arrested and killed, too.

Then Sunday morning happened.

The tomb was empty. Jesus was walking around, talking, and eating food. This wasn't just a plot twist; it was a total disruption of how the universe works. Because if dead people don't stay dead, then absolutely everything else Jesus said has to be true.

Big Idea

Jesus didn't just die for our sins; He physically rose from the dead, permanently defeating death and proving He is God.

Why This Matters

The resurrection is not a side detail of Christianity. It is the entire foundation.

If Jesus didn't rise from the dead, you should throw this book in the trash. Without an empty tomb, Jesus is just another dead martyr who made promises He couldn't keep.

- **It proves the payment cleared.** The resurrection was God the Father's way of publicly accepting Jesus' sacrifice on the cross.
- **It destroys the power of death.** Because Jesus beat the grave, death is no longer a permanent end for you; it is just a doorway.

Key Words

- **Resurrection:** A dead physical body returning to life, completely transformed and completely immortal.
- **Glorified Body:** The physical, physical, permanent body Jesus had after the resurrection, which could never die or get sick again.

- **Firstfruits:** A farming term used in the Bible to explain that Jesus' resurrection is the absolute guarantee that we will also be resurrected one day.

Precision Note (grown-up wording): The resurrection was not a *resuscitation* (like someone getting CPR and eventually dying again later); it was a permanent triumph over mortality.

Bible Receipts

The Apostle Paul refused to let Christians treat the resurrection as a cute metaphor.

He wrote a letter to a church in Corinth because some people were saying the physical resurrection wasn't a big deal. Paul essentially told them they were out of their minds.

He wrote, "And if Christ has not been raised, your faith is worthless; you are still in your sins" (1 Corinthians 15:17, CSB).

Paul stakes the entire Christian religion on this one historical event. If the tomb isn't empty, our faith is a joke. We are still guilty, and we have no hope for the future.

But Jesus went out of His way to prove He was actually alive. After He rose, He appeared to His disciples. They panicked, thinking He was a ghost. Jesus said to them, "'Look at my hands and my feet, that it is I myself! Touch me and see, because a ghost does not have flesh and bones as you can see I have.' ... They gave him a piece of a broiled fish, and he took it and ate in their presence" (Luke 24:39, 42-43, CSB).

Ghosts don't eat fish. Jesus wanted them to know His resurrection was physical, tangible, and real.

Truth in Plain English

Death has a 100% success rate against humanity. No amount of money, power, or technology has ever been able to stop it.

But Jesus defeated death from the inside out. When He went into the grave, He didn't stay there. He broke the jaws of death, kicked the doors of the tomb open, and walked out into the Sunday morning sun.

Highlightable line: The cross shows us the depth of God's love, but the empty tomb shows us the unstoppable power of God's victory.

Because Jesus conquered death, the worst thing that can happen to you is no longer the last thing that will happen to you. Jesus is the "firstfruits." He is the prototype. His resurrection guarantees that one day, when He returns, He is going to call your name and resurrect your physical body, too.

Common Confusion Box

Confusion #1: "The resurrection is just a spiritual metaphor about new beginnings." This sounds right because our culture loves stories about "rising from the ashes" or getting a fresh start. But it's wrong. The disciples didn't die for a metaphor. The Roman guards didn't panic over a metaphor. The tomb was physically empty. Jesus had real scars, He ate real food, and He was seen by over five hundred eyewitnesses at one time.

Highlightable line: Christianity isn't built on a spiritual feeling; it is built on the historical fact of an empty tomb.

Confusion #2: "People back then were gullible and didn't know dead people stay dead." This sounds right to modern skeptics who think ancient people were foolish and easily tricked by magic tricks. But here is what Scripture shows instead: Ancient people knew exactly how death worked. When Jesus died, Thomas (one of His closest friends) absolutely refused to believe He was alive until he could physically put his fingers into the scars on Jesus' hands. It took a literal miracle to convince them.

Why This Changes Real Life

The resurrection completely alters how you face the darkest moments of your life.

Eventually, you are going to stand at the edge of a grave. You will lose grandparents, friends, or parents. Death is the most brutal, painful enemy we face in this world. The grief can feel like it is going to completely crush you.

But because of the empty tomb, you do not have to grieve like the rest of the world.

You can stand at a cemetery with tears streaming down your face, but you don't have to despair. You know that the grave is not the end of the story. You know that the King you serve holds the keys to death, and He has promised to empty every single cemetery when He returns.

Highlightable line: Because the tomb is empty, your hope is secure.

Try This This Week

The "Empty Tomb" Anchor. When you feel overwhelmed with anxiety about the future or fear about a specific situation, say this out loud to yourself: *"If God can raise Jesus from the dead, He can handle this."* Let the biggest miracle in history shrink your current panic.

Talk It Out

- Why do you think the Apostle Paul said our faith is "worthless" if Jesus didn't physically rise from the dead?
- Why did Jesus go out of His way to eat broiled fish in front of His disciples after He resurrected?
- Read 1 Corinthians 15:17 again. How does the resurrection prove that our sins have actually been forgiven?
- How does the reality of the empty tomb change the way a Christian should experience a funeral?

BELIEF BUILDER (Brick #16: About Jesus)

My one-sentence belief: "I believe Jesus physically rose from the dead, permanently defeating death and proving He is the true Son of God."

Bible receipts (pick 1–2): 1 Corinthians 15:17; Luke 24:39

This changes my life because: "I do not have to fear death, because Jesus defeated it and promises to raise me to life as well."

One question I still have: (Write one honest question. No pretending.)

Short Prayer

Father, thank You that the grave could not hold Your Son. Jesus, You are the undisputed King who conquered death from the inside out. Holy Spirit, give me unshakable hope when I face loss and grief. Remind me that the worst thing is never the last thing. I praise You for the empty tomb. Amen.

My Notes & Thoughts

Brick #17: Jesus Now: King, Priest, Friend

Cold Open Moment

Where is Jesus right now?

If you had to draw a picture of what Jesus is doing at this exact second, what would you draw? Most people picture Him sitting on a fluffy cloud, staring at a giant clock, just waiting for God the Father to tell Him it's time to end the world. We treat Jesus like He is retired.

We know He was born in Bethlehem. We know He died on the cross. We know He rose from the dead. But we treat the last 2,000 years like Jesus is just sitting in heaven's waiting room, doing absolutely nothing.

If Jesus is inactive right now, you are on your own.

You have to fight your own temptations, defend your own failures, and somehow try to live the Christian life using your own willpower. But the Bible paints a completely different picture. Jesus didn't retire after the resurrection. He is aggressively, fiercely active in your life today.

Big Idea

Jesus is currently in heaven with a physical human body, actively ruling as King, praying for you as Priest, and walking with you as a Friend.

Why This Matters

Knowing what Jesus is doing right now changes how you survive Tuesday afternoon.

When you mess up and feel crushed by guilt, you need to know who is representing you in heaven. When you feel completely unseen and exhausted, you need to know who is watching over your life.

- **It gives you an Advocate.** You don't have to defend your own mistakes to God, because Jesus is doing it for you.
- **It grounds your humanity.** Because Jesus kept His human body, there is a real human being sitting on the throne of the universe right now.

Key Words

- **Ascension:** Forty days after the resurrection, Jesus physically went up into heaven in His glorified human body.
- **Intercession:** Praying on behalf of someone else; Jesus actively defending and advocating for you before the Father.
- **High Priest:** The ultimate mediator between God and humanity. Jesus bridges the gap perfectly.

- **Advocate:** Like a defense attorney, someone who stands beside you and fights for your case.

Precision Note (grown-up wording): Theologians talk about the *Session of Christ*, meaning Jesus is currently "seated at the right hand of the Father," indicating that His saving work is finished but His ruling work is ongoing.

Bible Receipts

The writer of Hebrews wanted desperate, struggling Christians to know exactly what Jesus was doing for them.

"Therefore, since we have a great high priest who has passed through the heavens, Jesus the Son of God, let us hold fast to our confession. For we do not have a high priest who is unable to sympathize with our weaknesses, but one who has been tempted in every way as we are, yet without sin" (Hebrews 4:14-15, CSB).

Jesus didn't drop His humanity when He went back to heaven. He is still fully human. He still remembers what it feels like to be exhausted, tempted, and betrayed.

And because He understands, He doesn't just sit there. The Apostle Paul tells us what Jesus is actually doing.

"Who is the one who condemns? Christ Jesus is the one who died, but even more, has been raised; he also is at the right hand of God and intercedes for us" (Romans 8:34, CSB).

If anyone had the right to condemn you, it would be Jesus. But instead of condemning you, He is currently using His authority to intercede, to pray and advocate, for you.

Truth in Plain English

Jesus is wearing three different hats for you right now.

First, He is your **King**. When He ascended to heaven, He sat down at the right hand of the Father. That is the seat of ultimate authority. He is actively directing history, managing the universe, and building His church. No politician or crisis can threaten His throne.

Second, He is your **Priest**. When the enemy accuses you of failing, Jesus acts as your defense attorney. He points to His scars and says to the Father, "That one belongs to me. Their debt is paid." You have the greatest Advocate in the universe fighting your case.

Highlightable line: You never have to defend yourself to God; you have a Savior who is praying for you at this very second.

Third, He is your **Friend**. Jesus isn't a distant boss. Through the Holy Spirit, He is present with you in the darkest, loneliest moments of your life. He sympathizes with your weakness because He actually knows what it feels like to be you.

Common Confusion Box

Confusion #1: "Jesus turned back into a pure spirit when He went to heaven." This sounds right because it is hard to imagine a physical human body existing in heaven. But it's wrong. When the disciples watched Jesus ascend into the clouds in Acts 1, He left in a physical body. He will return in a physical body. Right now, there is a glorified, scarred, human man reigning over the cosmos. Your humanity is permanently united to God.

Highlightable line. Jesus didn't just visit humanity; He permanently joined it.

Confusion #2: "I need to pray to saints or Mary so they can put in a good word for me with Jesus." This sounds right if you think Jesus is too busy, too holy, or too angry to listen to you directly. But here is what Scripture shows instead: 1 Timothy 2:5 says there is only *one* mediator between God and humanity, the man Christ Jesus. You don't need a middleman to get to the middleman. Jesus' door is always open.

Why This Changes Real Life

When you realize Jesus is actively interceding for you, the crushing weight of perfectionism finally breaks.

You are going to have days where your faith feels incredibly weak. You won't read your Bible. You will lose your temper. You will doubt if any of this is actually real. If Jesus is just a retired teacher, those days will ruin you.

But if Jesus is your High Priest, those are the days He is praying for you the hardest.

You don't have to clean yourself up before you talk to Him. You can walk boldly into His presence and say, "I am failing today, and I need help." He won't roll His eyes. He will sympathize with your weakness, apply the grace of His cross to your life, and give you the strength to keep going.

Highlightable line: When your prayers are weak, you are carried by the unstoppable prayers of Jesus.

Try This This Week

The "Advocate" Prayer. The next time you feel completely crushed by guilt over a mistake, don't hide. Pray this exactly: *"Jesus, the enemy is accusing me, and my own brain is accusing me. Thank You for being my Advocate and defending me right now."* ### Talk It Out

- Why do you think we tend to picture Jesus as "retired" or inactive in heaven?
- Read Hebrews 4:14-15 again. Why is it so important for us to know that Jesus still has a human nature right now?
- What is the difference between a King who just gives orders, and a High Priest who actually sympathizes with your weakness?
- How does knowing Jesus is actively praying for you change the way you handle guilt?

BELIEF BUILDER (Brick #17: About Jesus)

My one-sentence belief: "I believe Jesus ascended to heaven and is actively ruling as King, sympathizing with my weakness, and advocating for me as my High Priest."

Bible receipts (pick 1–2): Hebrews 4:14–15; Romans 8:34

This changes my life because: "I do not have to defend my own failures, because Jesus is constantly interceding for me."

One question I still have: (Write one honest question. No pretending.)

Short Prayer

Father, thank You that a human being currently sits on the throne of the universe. Jesus, thank You for perfectly defending my case when I stumble and fail. Holy Spirit, remind me that I am never fighting my battles alone. Give me the boldness to approach the throne of grace when I am weak. Thank You for being my King and my Friend. Amen.

My Notes & Thoughts

PART 4 - CHECKPOINT

Assemble Your Fourth Statement Section: "About Jesus"

You made it through Part 4. This is the absolute center of your theology. You've looked at the breathtaking reality of who Jesus is, what He did on the cross, His victory over the grave, and what He is doing right now.

It's time to stop reading and start building. In this checkpoint, you are going to cement your five new bricks into the most important paragraph of your Personal Statement of Faith.

Step 1: Gather Your Bricks

Look back at the Belief Builder sections from Chapters 13 through 17. Write your five one-sentence beliefs right here:

- **Brick 13 (God and Man):** ______________________________
- **Brick 14 (King and Savior):** ______________________________
- **Brick 15 (The Cross):** ______________________________
- **Brick 16 (The Resurrection):** ______________________________
- **Brick 17 (Ascension & Intercession):** ______________________________

Step 2: Edit for Power

If you stack all five of those sentences on top of each other, it will feel like a textbook. You need to smooth it out. Apply the **"Red Pen Rules"**:

1. **Keep the timeline clear.** Your paragraph should naturally flow from who He is, to His death, to His resurrection, to what He is doing now.
2. **Highlight the Great Exchange.** Make sure your sentence about the cross clearly explains *why* He died (as your substitute).
3. **Upgrade your vocabulary.** Circle and use your precision words: *divine*, *human*, *substitute*, *wrath*, *resurrected*, and *Advocate*.

Step 3: Draft Your Official Paragraph

Now, combine your edited bricks into one flowing, powerful paragraph. This is your personal confession about the Savior of the world.

My Statement of Faith: ABOUT JESUS

(Example Draft: "I believe Jesus Christ is the Son of God, fully divine and fully human. He did not just come to be a moral teacher, but to rescue me as Savior and rule as King. On the cross, He acted as my perfect substitute, absorbing God's holy wrath against my sin so I could receive His perfect righteousness. I believe He physically rose from the dead, permanently defeating death. He has ascended to heaven where He actively rules the universe and advocates for me as my High Priest.")

Step 4: The 10-Second Spoken Test

If someone asks you, "Who do you actually think Jesus is?" you can't just say, "He's a good guy." You need a clear, unshakeable script.

Look at your drafted paragraph and condense the massive theology into a single, spoken sentence.

My 10-Second Spoken Script:

"I believe Jesus is fully God and fully man, who died to pay for my sins, rose from the dead, and rules as King today."

Read your 10-second script out loud right now. Say it until you can look someone in the eye and speak it without hesitating.

Step 5: Log Your Receipts

You have massive theological claims in this section. Pick the **four strongest Bible verses** from Part 4 that back up your new paragraph, and write the references here.

1. ______________________________ (Example: John 1:1, 14 - Incarnation)
2. ______________________________ (Example: 2 Corinthians 5:21 - The Cross)
3. ______________________________ (Example: 1 Corinthians 15:17 - Resurrection)
4. ______________________________ (Example: Hebrews 4:14-15 - High Priest)

Congratulations. You have successfully defined the center of the Christian faith. You are ready for Part 5.

<u>My Statement of Faith (after part 4)</u>

PART 5 - SALVATION: Grace That Changes You

In this part, we're answering one of the biggest questions you'll ever ask: **How does someone get right with God, and what happens after that?** We'll walk through grace, faith, repentance, forgiveness, adoption, growth over time, and how assurance works when you don't feel spiritual. The goal is to help you write a "About Salvation" section that doesn't collapse into guilt or performance. By the end, you should be able to say, in your own words, what the gospel is, and why it's not "try harder," but a rescue that actually changes you.

Brick #18: Grace: Gift, Not Performance

Cold Open Moment

Your entire life is built on a scoreboard.

If you want to make the varsity team, you have to run faster and score more than the other players. If you want to get into a good college, you have to grind for a high GPA. If you want to get paid at a job, you have to show up and actually do the work.

Everything in our world operates on the law of performance: you get exactly what you earn.

So it makes complete sense that we drag this exact same mindset into our relationship with God. We subconsciously believe that God is holding a giant clipboard, tracking our good days and our bad days. We assume that if we read our Bibles, go to church, and avoid major sins, God owes us a good life and a ticket to heaven.

But if salvation is based on your performance, you are in massive trouble. Because no matter how hard you grind, you can never be perfect. The scoreboard will eventually crush you.

Big Idea

Salvation is a free gift of God's grace, entirely based on what Jesus earned for you, not what you earn for yourself.

Why This Matters

Understanding grace is the only way to get off the exhausting treadmill of religious performance.

If you think you have to earn your salvation, you will live in a constant state of anxiety. You will always wonder, *Did I do enough today? Is God mad at me? Did I just lose my salvation?* * **It destroys your pride.** You cannot brag about your faith, because you didn't achieve it; you just received it.

- **It destroys your despair.** You cannot be disqualified from a gift you never earned in the first place.

Key Words

- **Grace:** God's unmerited, unearned favor. It is getting an incredible gift that you do not deserve.
- **Works:** Any human effort, good deed, or religious activity done to try and earn God's approval.
- **Merit:** The concept of deserving a reward because of your good behavior.
- **The Gospel:** Literally "good news." It is the announcement of what Jesus has already done to save us.

Precision Note (grown-up wording): Theologians distinguish between *grace* (God giving us the good we don't deserve) and *merit* (humans attempting to achieve justification through works of the law).

Bible Receipts

The Apostle Paul is aggressively clear about how salvation actually works.

He writes to the church in Ephesus to make sure they don't take any credit for their rescue. "For you are saved by grace through faith, and this is not from yourselves; it is God's gift, not from works, so that no one can boast" (Ephesians 2:8-9, CSB).

Look at the words Paul uses. *Gift. Not from yourselves. Not from works.* If you work at a fast-food restaurant for forty hours, your boss hands you a paycheck. That isn't a gift; that is a wage you earned. But if a billionaire walks up to you on the street and hands you the keys to a brand new car, that is a gift.

Paul makes this exact comparison in Romans 11:6 (CSB): "Now if by grace, then it is not by works; otherwise grace ceases to be grace." Grace and human performance are like oil and water. They do not mix. You either earn it, or you are given it.

Truth in Plain English

Grace is the most scandalous, offensive concept in the history of religion.

Every other religion in the world gives you a ladder. They tell you to climb it through meditation, good deeds, or strict rules, and if you climb high enough, you might reach God.

Christianity tells you that the ladder is broken. You are paralyzed and cannot climb a single rung. So God climbed down the ladder to you, picked you up, and carried you to the top.

Highlightable line: Religion is spelled D-O; the Gospel is spelled D-O-N-E.

You do not get into heaven because you were the nicest kid in your high school. You get into heaven entirely because Jesus lived a perfect life in your place, and God credits His perfect score to your account for free.

Common Confusion Box

Confusion #1: "If grace is free, then I can just sin all I want and God will forgive me." This sounds right because if our behavior doesn't save us, it seems like our behavior doesn't matter at all. But it's wrong. True grace doesn't just forgive you; it transforms you. When you truly grasp the massive price Jesus paid to give you this free gift, your heart changes. You stop wanting to sin. You don't obey God to *earn* His love; you obey God because you *already have* His love.

Highlightable line: Grace isn't a license to live however you want; it is the power to finally live how you were designed.

Confusion #2: "God saves me by grace, but I have to keep myself saved by doing good works." This sounds right because we think God gives us a clean slate, but it is our job not to mess it up again. But here is what Scripture shows instead: Galatians 3 calls this foolishness. If you didn't have the power to save yourself on day one, you do not have the power to keep yourself saved on day one thousand. You are saved by grace, and you are sustained by grace.

Why This Changes Real Life

When grace actually clicks in your brain, it changes your entire personality.

You can finally drop the mask. In a world where everyone is exhausted from pretending to be perfect, you get to be honest. You can admit that you are messed up, that you struggle with anxiety, and that you fail your friends. You don't have to hide your flaws, because your flaws don't disqualify you from God's love.

It also makes you incredibly forgiving.

When someone wrongs you, it is easy to hold a grudge and demand that they pay you back. But when you realize that God has freely forgiven your massive, million-dollar debt of sin, it becomes much easier to forgive the ten-dollar debt someone else owes you.

Highlightable line: A person who has been wrecked by God's grace becomes a person who gives grace to everyone else.

Try This This Week

The "Zero Scoreboard" Morning. When you wake up tomorrow, before your feet even touch the floor, say this out loud: *"I have a perfect score with God today, and I haven't done a single thing to earn it."* Let grace set the tone for your entire day.

Talk It Out

- Why is it so incredibly hard for human beings to accept a completely free gift without trying to pay for it?
- Read Ephesians 2:8-9 again. Why does Paul specifically add the phrase "so that no one can boast"?
- How does the "ladder" analogy help explain the difference between Christianity and every other world religion?
- If you truly believed that God's love for you is not based on your performance, how would that change your anxiety levels this week?

BELIEF BUILDER (Brick #18: About Salvation)

My one-sentence belief: "I believe salvation is a completely free gift of God's grace, entirely earned by Jesus, and cannot be achieved by my own good works."

Bible receipts (pick 1–2): Ephesians 2:8–9; Romans 11:6

This changes my life because: "I can step off the exhausting treadmill of trying to be perfect and just rest in what Jesus has done for me."

One question I still have: (Write one honest question. No pretending.)

Short Prayer

Father, thank You for climbing down the ladder to save me when I was completely stuck. Jesus, thank You for doing all the work and giving me all the credit. Holy Spirit, whenever I try to earn my way back into Your favor, remind me of the cross. Kill my pride. Help me to live a life of joy and obedience because I am already loved. Amen.

My Notes & Thoughts

Brick #19: Faith and Repentance (real trust)

Cold Open Moment

Imagine you are standing on the edge of an airplane, 10,000 feet in the air, wearing a parachute.

The instructor asks you, "Do you believe this parachute will save your life?" You enthusiastically nod. You have read the manual. You know the parachute was packed correctly. You mentally agree with all the facts about the parachute.

But if you turn around, walk back to your seat, and buckle your seatbelt, did you actually have faith in the parachute? No. You only had an intellectual opinion about it.

We do the exact same thing with Jesus. Millions of people mentally agree that Jesus is the Son of God. They check the "Christian" box on surveys. They believe *about* Jesus, but they have never actually put their weight on Him.

If you want the parachute to save you, you have to jump. And in Christianity, jumping looks like two very specific actions: faith and repentance.

Big Idea

To be saved, you must turn away from your rebellion (repentance) and actively put your full trust in Jesus (faith).

Why This Matters

This is where the rubber meets the road. Grace is the free gift, but faith and repentance are how you actually open the box and receive the gift.

If you get this wrong, you will end up with "easy believism", a fake version of Christianity where you say a quick prayer to avoid hell, but your life never actually changes.

- **It proves your faith is real.** A faith that doesn't change your direction is a faith that cannot save your soul.
- **It gives you a clear response.** You don't have to guess what God wants you to do; He clearly commands you to repent and believe.

Key Words

- **Repentance:** A radical change of mind and heart that leads to a radical change in direction. It is turning away from sin.
- **Faith:** Not just intellectual agreement, but actively trusting and relying on Jesus Christ alone to save you.
- **Conversion:** The moment when the Holy Spirit brings you from spiritual death to spiritual life, marked by your

repentance and faith.

- **Fruit:** The visible, external evidence in your life that your internal faith is actually real.

Precision Note (grown-up wording): Theologians consider faith and repentance to be two sides of the same coin, often referring to them together as *conversion*. You cannot turn toward Christ without simultaneously turning away from sin.

Bible Receipts

When Jesus began His public ministry, He didn't tell people to just "be nice" or "try harder." He gave a very specific command.

"The time is fulfilled, and the kingdom of God has come near. Repent and believe the good news!" (Mark 1:15, CSB).

Notice the two commands: Repent and believe. They are a package deal. You cannot truly believe the good news while refusing to repent of the bad news.

But what does this belief actually look like? James, the half-brother of Jesus, wrote a letter to clear up the confusion about fake faith.

He wrote, "You believe that God is one. Good! Even the demons believe, and they shudder" (James 2:19, CSB).

Demons have excellent theology. They know exactly who Jesus is. They know He died on the cross and rose from the dead. But demons are not saved, because they refuse to submit to Him. Mental agreement is not enough. James concludes, "For just as the body without the spirit is dead, so also faith without works is dead" (James 2:26, CSB).

Truth in Plain English

Repentance and faith are two sides of the exact same coin.

Imagine you are driving a car 90 miles per hour down the highway, heading straight for a cliff. Repentance is hitting the brakes, grabbing the steering wheel, and doing a massive U-turn. You are changing your mind about the direction you were going.

Highlightable line: Repentance isn't just feeling sorry that you got caught; it is a genuine hatred of the sin that is destroying you.

But you can't just do a U-turn and sit in the middle of the road. You have to drive in a new direction. That is faith. Faith is putting your foot on the gas and driving directly toward Jesus.

You aren't saved *because* you do a U-turn perfectly. You are saved because Jesus is the one holding you. But the U-turn is the undeniable proof that you have actually realized who Jesus is.

Common Confusion Box

Confusion #1: "I have to clean up my life and fix my habits before I can repent." This sounds right because we think we need to present a clean version of ourselves to God. But it's wrong. You do not clean yourself up before you jump into the shower; you jump into the shower *so* you can get clean. Repentance isn't fixing yourself; it is dragging your broken, messy, addicted self to Jesus and asking Him to do the fixing.

Highlightable line: God doesn't demand that you are perfect before you come to Him; He just demands that you are honest.

Confusion #2: "Faith is just blindly hoping something is true even when there is no evidence." This sounds right because culture defines faith as a blind leap in the dark. But here is what Scripture shows instead: Biblical faith is not blind. It is a calculated trust based on a reliable track record. You trust Jesus with your soul the same way you trust a pilot with your life, not blindly, but because the pilot has proven he knows how to fly the plane. Jesus proved His reliability by walking out of an empty tomb.

Why This Changes Real Life

When you understand real faith and repentance, it frees you from the trap of fake Christianity.

There are thousands of teenagers sitting in youth groups who are utterly miserable because they are playing a game. They raised their hand at a camp fire, but they never actually repented. They are trying to hold onto Jesus with one hand while holding onto their favorite, secret sins with the other hand.

That will tear you apart. You cannot walk in two opposite directions at the same time.

But when you finally let go of your sin, when you actually repent, the relief is unbelievable. You aren't playing a game anymore. You have jumped out of the airplane, and you discover that the parachute actually holds your weight.

Highlightable line: Real faith isn't about perfectly understanding everything; it is about completely trusting the One who does.

Try This This Week

The "Drop It" Prayer. Identify one specific habit, attitude, or secret sin in your life right now that you know is rebellion. Get on your knees in your bedroom, open your hands, and pray: *"Jesus, I am turning away from this, and I am turning toward You. I trust You more than I trust this sin."*

Talk It Out

- What is the difference between feeling guilty about a sin, and actually repenting of it?
- Read James 2:19 again. Why is it so shocking to realize that demons have "perfect theology"? What are they missing?
- How does the parachute analogy explain the difference between mental agreement and saving faith?
- Why is it impossible to have real faith in Jesus without also experiencing repentance?

BELIEF BUILDER (Brick #19: About Salvation)

My one-sentence belief: "I believe that to be saved, I must turn away from my sin in repentance and put my full, active trust in Jesus Christ alone."

Bible receipts (pick 1–2): Mark 1:15; James 2:19

This changes my life because: "I know my faith isn't just a mental opinion, but a real relationship that completely changes my direction."

One question I still have: (Write one honest question. No pretending.)

Short Prayer

Father, thank You for the gift of true faith. Jesus, I am dropping my rebellion and putting my full weight on Your promises. Holy Spirit, give me a genuine hatred for my sin and a deep love for the truth. When I am tempted to just play religious games, pull me back to real repentance. Keep me walking in Your direction. Amen.

My Notes & Thoughts

Brick #20: Justification and Forgiveness (new status)

Cold Open Moment

You know the absolute dread of getting caught.

Maybe you cheated on a massive final exam, or you lied about where you were on a Friday night, or you said something incredibly cruel behind a friend's back. And then, the text message comes. *We need to talk.* Your stomach instantly drops. You are walking into the principal's office or sitting down at the kitchen table with your parents, and you know you are completely guilty. You have no defense. You are just waiting for the hammer to drop. You are waiting for the punishment, the grounding, the permanent mark on your record.

When we think about standing before God, we usually feel that exact same dread. We know our own thoughts. We know our own secrets. We know our record is a complete disaster.

But what if the Judge didn't just let you off with a warning? What if the Judge took your permanent record, threw it in a shredder, and then legally declared that you were the best citizen in the history of the universe?

Big Idea

When you trust in Jesus, God completely forgives your debt of sin and legally declares you perfectly righteous.

Why This Matters

This is the doctrine that lets you sleep at night.

If you are not justified, your relationship with God is always on probation. You will constantly feel like you are one major mistake away from being kicked out of the family.

- **It crushes condemnation.** The enemy can no longer use your past against you, because your past has been legally erased.
- **It gives you unshakeable confidence.** You don't have to wonder if you are going to heaven, because your status is guaranteed by God's legal decree.

Key Words

- **Forgiveness:** God wiping away the massive debt of sin that you owed Him. You are no longer in the negative.
- **Justification:** God legally declaring you to be perfectly righteous in His sight. You are now fully in the positive.
- **Condemnation:** The guilty verdict and the legal punishment for sin.

- **Righteousness:** A status of perfect moral purity and right standing before God.

Precision Note (grown-up wording): Justification is a *forensic* (legal) act of God. It is an instant change in our legal status before the Judge, not a gradual process of us getting better over time.

Bible Receipts

The Apostle Paul wrote the book of Romans to explain exactly how this legal transaction works.

He sets up the absolute best news in the world in Romans 8:1 (CSB): "Therefore, there is now no condemnation for those in Christ Jesus."

Zero. None. Not a little bit of condemnation on your bad days. If you are "in Christ," the gavel has struck, and the sentence of condemnation has been permanently canceled.

But how can a holy Judge do that without ignoring the law? Paul explains it earlier in Romans 3:24 (CSB): "They are justified freely by his grace through the redemption that is in Christ Jesus."

We are justified *freely*. You don't pay for it. Jesus paid the fine on the cross, and because the fine is paid, the Judge has the legal right to declare you innocent. God didn't sweep your sin under the rug; He dealt with it legally on the cross, allowing Him to justify you immediately.

Truth in Plain English

Forgiveness and justification are two different things, and you desperately need both of them.

Imagine you owe the bank one million dollars. You are completely bankrupt. Forgiveness is the bank manager calling you and saying, "We wiped out your debt. You owe us nothing." That is incredible news! You are no longer in debt. Your balance is zero.

But having a zero balance doesn't make you rich. It just means you aren't drowning anymore.

Highlightable line: Forgiveness wipes out your massive debt, but justification deposits a billion dollars into your account.

Justification is God taking the perfect, flawless, million-dollar record of Jesus Christ's life and legally transferring it into your bank account. When God the Father looks at you now, He does not see your blank, zero-balance record. He sees the perfect righteousness of His own Son.

Common Confusion Box

Confusion #1: "Justification means God instantly makes me act like a perfect person." This sounds right because if God declares us righteous, we assume we should immediately stop sinning. But it's wrong. Justification is a change in your *status*, not an instant change in your *behavior*. If a judge legally declares you debt-free, you might still have the bad habit of spending too much money. You still have to grow and fight sin, but you do it from a legally secure position.

Highlightable line: Justification doesn't mean you are suddenly flawless; it means God legally views you through the flawless lens of Jesus.

Confusion #2: "I still feel so guilty about my past, so God must still be holding it against me." This sounds right because our emotions are incredibly powerful, and shame lingers long after a mistake. But here is what Scripture shows instead: Your legal status in God's courtroom is not determined by your emotional state. If the Judge has declared "Not Guilty," it doesn't matter if you still feel guilty. The verdict is final. Your feelings don't overrule God's gavel.

Why This Changes Real Life

Understanding justification is the ultimate cure for shame.

When you define yourself by your worst mistake, the text you shouldn't have sent, the party you shouldn't have gone to, the lie you told your parents, you walk around with a heavy, invisible label on your forehead that says *Guilty*. You expect people to reject you.

Justification rips that label off.

It tells you that you are not your worst mistake. You are not your darkest secret. Your identity is fundamentally and legally anchored in what Jesus did for you. You are accepted. You are clean.

Highlightable line: Because of justification, you don't have to defend your reputation anymore; Jesus is your reputation.

Try This This Week

The "Gavel Strike." Sometime this week, when your brain brings up a cringy, shameful memory from your past to make you feel guilty, physically clap your hands together once (like a gavel). Say out loud: *"No condemnation. The case is closed."*

Talk It Out

- What is the difference between having your debt "forgiven" (zero balance) and being "justified" (credited with Christ's righteousness)?
- Read Romans 8:1 again. Why is the word "now" so important in that verse?
- Why is it so dangerous to let our feelings of guilt overrule God's legal declaration of "not guilty"?
- If you truly believed that God viewed you as perfectly righteous, how would you respond the next time you messed up?

BELIEF BUILDER (Brick #20: About Salvation)

My one-sentence belief: "I believe that through faith in Jesus, my sins are completely forgiven and God legally declares me to be perfectly righteous."

Bible receipts (pick 1–2): Romans 8:1; Romans 3:24

This changes my life because: "I do not have to live under the crushing weight of shame and condemnation anymore."

One question I still have: (Write one honest question. No pretending.)

Short Prayer

Father, thank You for throwing my permanent record in the shredder. Jesus, thank You for giving me Your perfect righteousness when I had absolutely nothing to offer. Holy Spirit, when the enemy tries to drag me back into the courtroom of shame, remind me of Romans 8:1. Help me to live in the massive freedom of being completely justified. Amen.

My Notes & Thoughts

Brick #21: Adoption (belonging)

Cold Open Moment

You know the feeling of walking into a crowded cafeteria and not knowing where to sit.

You scan the room, looking at the different tables, desperately hoping someone will make eye contact and slide over to make room for you. You don't want to just exist in the room; you want to actually belong. We all have a deep, hardwired craving to be chosen, to be wanted, and to be part of a family.

For a lot of people, the idea of God feels like a boss who finally agreed to hire you, or a judge who finally agreed to let you out of jail.

But a judge doesn't invite you over for Thanksgiving dinner. A boss doesn't hold you when you cry. If your relationship with God stops at forgiveness, you will always feel like an outsider who is just lucky to be in the building.

But God didn't just forgive you. He gave you a seat at the table.

Big Idea

When you trust in Jesus, God doesn't just forgive your sins; He officially adopts you into His family with all the rights of a true child.

Why This Matters

Adoption changes the entire vibe of your relationship with God.

If you view God as your boss, you will only talk to Him when you want a promotion or when you are in trouble. But if you view God as your Father, you can talk to Him about absolutely anything.

- **It gives you unshakeable belonging.** You don't have to hustle to fit in, because the Creator of the universe already chose you.
- **It changes how you view other Christians.** They aren't just people who go to the same building as you; they are literally your eternal brothers and sisters.

Key Words

- **Adoption:** The legal act of God making us members of His own family, giving us all the privileges of His children.
- **Orphan:** Someone who is spiritually alone, trying to survive and provide for themselves without a Father.
- **Heir:** A child who has the legal right to inherit the wealth and kingdom of their father.

- **Abba:** An intimate, Aramaic term for "father," very similar to "Dad" or "Papa."

Precision Note (grown-up wording): Theologians clarify that *justification* is about our legal standing before a Judge, while *adoption* goes a step further and establishes our personal relationship with a Father.

Bible Receipts

The Apostle Paul loved the concept of adoption because he knew it was the ultimate proof of God's love.

He wrote to the Romans, "For you did not receive a spirit of slavery to fall back into fear. Instead, you received the Spirit of adoption, by whom we cry out, 'Abba, Father!'" (Romans 8:15, CSB).

Slaves live in constant fear of messing up and getting fired. Children don't. When a toddler falls down, they don't hide from their dad out of fear; they cry out for their dad to pick them up.

Paul takes it even further in the book of Galatians. "But when the time came to completion, God sent his Son... so that we might receive adoption as sons" (Galatians 4:4-5, CSB).

And because we are sons and daughters, God gives us the ultimate family inheritance. Galatians 4:7 says, "So you are no longer a slave but a son, and if a son, then God has made you an heir."

Truth in Plain English

It is one thing for a judge to look at a guilty criminal, pay their fine, and let them walk out of the courtroom free. That is justification.

But it is a completely different thing for that same judge to step down from the bench, walk over to the criminal, and say, "I'm taking you home. You are going to live in my house, eat my food, and carry my last name."

Highlightable line: Justification means God won't punish you; adoption means God actually wants you.

When you are adopted by God, you get full access. You don't have to schedule an appointment to talk to the King of the universe. You can walk right into the throne room in the middle of a math test because you are a child of the King.

Common Confusion Box

Confusion #1: "Isn't everyone in the world automatically a child of God?" This sounds right because God created every human being, and we like the idea that everyone is in the same family. But it's wrong. The Bible teaches that everyone is a *creation* of God, but we are not naturally born as *children* of God. Because of our sin, we are actually born completely separated from Him. You only become a child of God when you are spiritually adopted into the family through faith in Jesus.

Highlightable line: You were created by God on your actual birthday, but you are adopted by God on your spiritual birthday.

Confusion #2: "If my earthly dad was distant or abusive, God is probably the same way." This sounds right because our earthly parents are the first lens we look through to understand what a "father" is. But here is what Scripture shows instead: Your earthly dad is a broken, flawed human. God is not a bigger version of your earthly dad; God is the perfect Father your heart has always been searching for. He is the Father who never leaves, never breaks a promise, and never loses His temper.

Why This Changes Real Life

When you actually grasp your adoption, it destroys the orphan mindset.

An orphan mindset says, "I am on my own. I have to fight for everything I get. If I don't protect myself, nobody else will." A lot of Christians still live this way. They live with extreme anxiety about their future, their money, and their reputation, because they think they are the only ones looking out for them.

But a child with a good Father lives differently.

When you know you are adopted by God, you can relax. You know that your Father owns the universe. He knows what you need before you even ask Him. You don't have to claw your way to the top or panic when things go wrong, because your Dad is fiercely protective of His kids.

Highlightable line: You can stop living like a spiritual orphan trying to survive, and start living like a royal heir who is perfectly safe.

Try This This Week

The "Abba" Prayer. Sometime this week, change the way you normally start your prayers. Instead of saying "Dear God" or "Lord," start your prayer by saying, *"Abba, Father."* Speak to Him with the absolute confidence of a child talking to a Dad who loves them.

Talk It Out

- What is the biggest difference between treating God like a boss versus treating Him like a Father?
- Read Romans 8:15 again. Why do you think Paul contrasts the "spirit of slavery" directly with the "Spirit of adoption"?
- How does the idea of spiritual adoption change the way you view the older, weirder, or totally different people in your church?
- If you truly believed God was your perfect, protective Father, what is one area of anxiety you would finally let go of?

BELIEF BUILDER (Brick #21: About Salvation)

My one-sentence belief: "I believe that when I trusted Jesus, God officially adopted me into His family, making me His child and giving me total access to Him."

Bible receipts (pick 1–2): Romans 8:15; Galatians 4:4–7

This changes my life because: "I don't have to live like an orphan fighting for survival; I am a chosen and loved child of the King."

One question I still have: (Write one honest question. No pretending.)

Short Prayer

Abba, Father, thank You for wanting me in Your family. Jesus, thank You for sharing Your inheritance with me. Holy Spirit, when I feel like an outsider, remind me that I belong at the table. Heal the wounds left by the broken people in my life. Help me to fully trust my perfect Heavenly Father. Amen.

My Notes & Thoughts

Brick #22: Sanctification (growth over time)

Cold Open Moment

It happens to almost everyone after a massive spiritual high.

Maybe you went to a summer camp, cried during the worship music, and made a huge commitment to God. Or maybe you just got baptized. You felt totally clean, completely focused, and you swore to yourself, *I am never going back to my old habits. I am a completely new person.* And then Tuesday rolls around.

You lose your temper with your mom. You click on a website you swore you would never visit again. You join in on the cafeteria gossip. Suddenly, the spiritual high is completely gone, and a terrifying thought hits you: *Why am I still doing this? Did my salvation even work?* We expect instant perfection. But God usually doesn't work through instant magic tricks; He works through a slow, messy, lifelong process.

Big Idea

Sanctification is the lifelong, often messy process of the Holy Spirit slowly changing your desires and making you look more like Jesus.

Why This Matters

If you don't understand how sanctification works, you will probably quit Christianity out of pure frustration.

You will think that your continued struggle with sin means God has abandoned you. But understanding this process gives you the endurance to keep fighting, even when you lose a battle.

- **It gives you patience.** You realize that spiritual growth is a marathon, not a teleportation.
- **It proves you are alive.** Dead things don't fight back. The fact that you are currently struggling against your sin proves the Holy Spirit is actually inside you.

Key Words

- **Sanctification:** The ongoing process of becoming holy and being transformed into the image of Christ.
- **Mortification:** The aggressive, daily habit of putting your sinful desires to death.
- **Transformation:** A complete change of your internal nature, not just behavior modification.
- **Fruit of the Spirit:** The natural results of the Holy Spirit working in your life (love, joy, peace, patience, kindness).

Precision Note (grown-up wording): Theologians distinguish between *definitive sanctification* (you are permanently set apart for God the moment you are saved) and *progressive sanctification* (you gradually grow in holiness over your entire life).

Bible Receipts

The Apostle Paul knew that Christians were going to get easily discouraged with their own slow progress.

So he wrote a promise to the church in Philippi: "I am sure of this, that he who started a good work in you will carry it on to completion until the day of Christ Jesus" (Philippians 1:6, CSB).

Notice who is doing the heavy lifting. *He* started it. *He* will carry it on. You are not left alone to fix yourself. The Holy Spirit is actively renovating your heart, and He does not abandon His construction projects halfway through.

But you still have a massive role to play in this process.

Paul commands the Romans, "Do not be conformed to this age, but be transformed by the renewing of your mind, so that you may discern what is the good, pleasing, and perfect will of God" (Romans 12:2, CSB).

You don't just sit on the couch and wait to become holy. You have to actively fight. You have to renew your mind by spending time in God's word and refusing to let the culture shape your brain.

Truth in Plain English

When you are saved, God gives you a new heart, but you still have your old habits.

Think of it like buying a house that has been totally trashed. The moment you sign the papers, the house is legally yours (justification). But it takes months of smashing walls, ripping up gross carpet, and painting over ugly colors to make the house beautiful (sanctification).

Highlightable line: Justification happens in a single moment; sanctification takes an entire lifetime.

As you grow, your desires actually start to change. The sins you used to love start to taste bitter. The things of God that used to bore you start to feel beautiful. You won't reach total perfection until you get to heaven, but you should absolutely look more like Jesus this year than you did last year.

Common Confusion Box

Confusion #1: "If I'm saved by grace, I don't need to try hard to be good." This sounds right if you think grace is just a get-out-of-jail-free card that requires zero effort. But it's wrong. The Bible commands us to actively fight sin. Paul says to "put to death" the sinful things in us. Grace isn't an excuse to be lazy; grace is the fuel that gives you the power to actually fight. You are not fighting *for* your salvation; you are fighting *from* your salvation.

Highlightable line: Effort does not equal earning. God demands your effort, but your effort does not earn His love.

Confusion #2: "If I still struggle with a specific sin, I must not be a real Christian." This sounds right because we assume real Christians have it all together. But here is what Scripture shows instead: The Apostle Paul himself wrote agonizingly about his own daily struggle with sin in Romans 7. The presence of a struggle isn't proof you are unsaved; it is proof you are at war. Unsaved people don't go to war with their sin; they just surrender to it.

Why This Changes Real Life

Sanctification completely changes how you view your own failures.

When you stumble back into a bad habit, the enemy wants you to throw your hands up, say "I guess I'm a fake," and quit completely. But when you understand that sanctification is a process, a failure doesn't destroy you.

You can get up, repent, and realize that getting back in the fight is exactly what a Christian does.

It also changes how you view the other people in your church. When you see a Christian act like a total hypocrite, you don't have to throw your faith away. You realize that they are a house under construction, too. Some rooms are painted, and some rooms are still a total disaster. You can give them the exact same patience that God gives you.

Highlightable line: God is infinitely more patient with your slow growth than you are.

Try This This Week

The "Replace It" Rule. Sanctification isn't just stopping bad things; it is starting good things. Pick one bad habit you are trying to kill this week (like scrolling when you feel anxious). Decide right now what healthy, Jesus-honoring habit you will *replace* it with (like texting an encouraging word to a friend or reading a Psalm).

Talk It Out

- Why do you think we expect instant spiritual perfection from ourselves, even though we know we are flawed?
- Read Philippians 1:6 again. Why is it a massive relief to know that *God* is the one who promises to finish the work in you?
- Look at the house analogy. What is one "room" in your life that God is currently trying to renovate?
- What is the difference between fighting sin to *earn* God's love, and fighting sin *because* you already have God's love?

BELIEF BUILDER (Brick #22: About the Christian Life)

My one-sentence belief: "I believe sanctification is the lifelong, everyday process of the Holy Spirit actively transforming my heart and habits to look more like Jesus."

Bible receipts (pick 1–2): Philippians 1:6; Romans 12:2

This changes my life because: "I can be patient with my own slow growth and refuse to give up when I fail a battle."

One question I still have: (Write one honest question. No pretending.)

Short Prayer

Father, thank You for not leaving me the way You found me. Jesus, thank You for providing the perfect model of what a human life should look like. Holy Spirit, give me the grit and the power to aggressively fight my sin today. When I fail, give me the courage to get back up. Please finish the good work You started in me. Amen.

My Notes & Thoughts

Brick #23: Assurance (can I know?)

Cold Open Moment

Almost every Christian has prayed "the prayer" more than once.

You know the one. You are lying in bed at night, staring at the ceiling, and a wave of pure panic hits your chest. You think back to the time you asked Jesus to save you, and you start analyzing the moment.

Did I mean it enough? Did I use the right words? What if I was just emotional because the music was playing? What if God didn't actually hear me?

So, just to be safe, you pray the prayer again. "God, if I didn't actually mean it the first time, I am asking You to save me right now. For real this time."

You fall asleep feeling a little better, but three months later, you make a massive mistake, the guilt rushes back, and you pray the exact same prayer again. You are caught in a terrifying cycle of "spiritual amnesia," constantly wondering if your salvation was a fluke.

If you can't be sure you are saved, your faith will always be paralyzed by fear.

Big Idea

Your salvation is secured by Jesus' perfect grip on you, not your fragile grip on Him, meaning you can have absolute assurance.

Why This Matters

Assurance is the oxygen of the Christian life.

You cannot grow, serve, or take bold risks for God if you are constantly terrified that He is holding a trapdoor lever under your feet.

- **It gives you peace.** You don't have to wake up every morning wondering if you are still in the family.
- **It redirects your focus.** Instead of constantly staring at your own messy heart to find proof of salvation, you learn to stare at the finished work of Jesus.

Key Words

- **Assurance:** The confident, unshakeable inner knowledge that you are truly saved and belong to God.
- **Preservation:** The promise that God will actively protect and keep His true children saved forever.

- **Perseverance:** The reality that a true Christian will continue to believe and follow Jesus to the very end of their life.
- **Doubt:** A feeling of uncertainty, which is a normal human struggle and not the same thing as unbelief.

Precision Note (grown-up wording): Theologians call this the *Perseverance of the Saints*, meaning that those who are truly justified by God can never fully or finally fall away from grace, but will be kept by His power unto the end.

Bible Receipts

Jesus spoke directly to the people who were terrified of losing their salvation.

He used the analogy of a shepherd protecting his sheep. "My sheep hear my voice, I know them, and they follow me. I give them eternal life, and they will never perish. No one will snatch them out of my hand" (John 10:27-28, CSB).

Jesus doesn't say, "They will never perish... unless they really mess up on a Tuesday." He says no one can snatch them out of His hand. You are not strong enough to break the grip of the Son of God.

The Apostle John wrote an entire letter to a church that was struggling with major doubts. He ends his letter with this bold statement: "I have written these things to you who believe in the name of the Son of God so that you may know that you have eternal life" (1 John 5:13, CSB).

God doesn't want you to guess. He doesn't want you to just hope you make the cut. He wants you to *know* that you have eternal life right now.

Truth in Plain English

The reason you doubt your salvation is because you are looking in the wrong direction.

When you wonder if you are saved, you usually look inward. You look at your recent track record, your emotional intensity, and your current level of obedience. Because your heart is messy and your emotions constantly change, your assurance constantly changes.

But assurance isn't found by looking at yourself. It is found by looking at the object of your faith.

Highlightable line: A weak faith in a strong bridge will still get you across the canyon; a strong faith in a rotten bridge will get you killed.

Your salvation does not depend on the flawless intensity of your faith. It depends entirely on the flawless perfection of Jesus. If you have placed your tiny, mustard-seed-sized faith in the massive, finished work of the cross, you are completely secure.

Common Confusion Box

Confusion #1: "If I feel distant from God, I must have lost my salvation." This sounds right because we live in a culture that worships feelings. If we don't *feel* saved, we assume we aren't. But it's wrong. Your salvation is a legal, objective fact based on the cross, not a subjective feeling based on your mood. Just like you are still legally your parents' child even on the days you are angry with them, you are still God's child even when your emotions are entirely numb.

Highlightable line: Stop checking your emotional pulse to see if you are spiritually alive; check the empty tomb.

Confusion #2: "I know a guy who was a hardcore Christian, but he completely walked away and hates God now. Didn't he lose his salvation?" This sounds right because we see people "deconstruct" and abandon their faith all the time. But here is what Scripture shows instead: 1 John 2:19 addresses this exactly. "They went out from us, but they did not belong to us; for if they had belonged to us, they would have remained with us." If someone totally and permanently abandons Jesus, they didn't lose their salvation; they just proved they never actually had it in the first place.

Why This Changes Real Life

When you finally settle the question of your salvation, you become incredibly dangerous to the enemy.

If the devil can keep you obsessing over whether or not you are actually saved, he can keep you completely sidelined. You will be too busy analyzing your own heart to ever share the gospel with a friend, serve the poor, or take a risk for the Kingdom.

But when you lock in your assurance, that anxiety evaporates.

You can walk into your school knowing that the biggest question of your existence has already been answered. Your eternal future is permanently sealed. You don't have to live in fear. You get to live in absolute freedom.

Highlightable line: True assurance doesn't make you arrogant; it makes you incredibly grateful and utterly fearless.

Try This This Week

The "Outside Voice" Habit. When a massive wave of doubt hits you late at night, your internal voice is going to lie to you. You have to fight it with an external voice. Sometime this week, physically read John 10:28 out loud. Tell your brain exactly whose hand is holding you.

Talk It Out

- Have you ever prayed the "did I really mean it?" prayer multiple times? Why do you think that is such a common experience?
- Read John 10:27-28 again. How does the image of being inside the hand of Jesus change the way you view your security?
- Why is it so dangerous to base our assurance of salvation on how we feel on any given day?
- How does the bridge analogy help explain that the *object* of your faith is more important than the *amount* of your faith?

BELIEF BUILDER (Brick #23: About Salvation)

My one-sentence belief: "I believe my salvation is eternally secure, not because my faith is perfect, but because Jesus' grip on me is unbreakable."

Bible receipts (pick 1–2): John 10:27–28; 1 John 5:13

This changes my life because: "I can stop living in terror of losing my salvation and start living in the freedom of His permanent love."

One question I still have: (Write one honest question. No pretending.)

Short Prayer

Father, thank You for wanting me to have absolute confidence in Your love. Jesus, thank You for promising that no one can ever snatch me out of Your hand. Holy Spirit, when my feelings tell me I am lost, anchor my mind to the facts of the Gospel. Help me to stop looking at my own weak faith, and start staring at my strong Savior. Amen.

My Notes & Thoughts

PART 5 - CHECKPOINT

Assemble Your Fifth Statement Section: "About Salvation"

You made it through Part 5. This section was massive. You covered the free gift of grace, the necessity of real faith, the legal declaration of your innocence, your adoption into the family, the messy process of growing, and the absolute security of your soul.

It is time to cement these truths together. This is the paragraph where you declare exactly how a broken human being gets rescued by a holy God.

Step 1: Gather Your Bricks

Look back at the Belief Builder sections from Chapters 18 through 23. Write your six one-sentence beliefs right here:

- **Brick 18 (Grace):** ______________________________
- **Brick 19 (Faith & Repentance):** ______________________________
- **Brick 20 (Justification):** ______________________________
- **Brick 21 (Adoption):** ______________________________
- **Brick 22 (Sanctification):** ______________________________
- **Brick 23 (Assurance):** ______________________________

Step 2: Edit for Power

This is a lot of theology to fit into one paragraph. You have to be brutal with your editing. Apply the **"Red Pen Rules"**:

1. **Follow the logical order.** Start with the free gift (grace/faith), move to the instant results (justification/adoption), and end with the ongoing realities (sanctification/assurance).
2. **Combine related concepts.** You can easily combine Justification and Adoption into one strong sentence (e.g., "God legally forgives me and permanently adopts me...").
3. **Upgrade your vocabulary.** Make sure your paragraph features the heavy-hitting words: *grace*, *repentance*, *justified*, *adopted*, *sanctified*, and *secure*.

Step 3: Draft Your Official Paragraph

Now, combine your edited bricks into one flowing paragraph. Make it read like a bold declaration of freedom.

My Statement of Faith: ABOUT SALVATION

(Example Draft: "I believe salvation is a completely free gift of God's grace, earned by Jesus and received when I turn from sin in repentance and trust in Him. Through faith, my sins are completely forgiven, and God justifies me, legally declaring me righteous. I am officially adopted into God's family as a loved child. The Holy Spirit then begins the lifelong process of sanctification, slowly changing my habits to look like Jesus. My salvation is eternally secure, held not by my perfect performance, but by Christ's unbreakable grip.")

Step 4: The 10-Second Spoken Test

If someone asks you, "So, what do you actually have to do to be saved?" you need an answer that is instantly clear and totally free of religious jargon.

Look at your drafted paragraph and condense it into a single, spoken script.

My 10-Second Spoken Script:

"I believe I am saved by God's free grace when I repent and trust in Jesus, making me fully forgiven, adopted, and permanently secure."

Read your 10-second script out loud right now. Practice it until you can say it with unshakeable confidence.

Step 5: Log Your Receipts

Pick the **four strongest Bible verses** from Part 5 that back up your new paragraph, and write the references here.

1. ________________________________ (Example: Ephesians 2:8-9 - Grace)
2. ________________________________ (Example: Mark 1:15 - Repentance & Faith)
3. ________________________________ (Example: Romans 8:1 - Justification)
4. ________________________________ (Example: John 10:27-28 - Assurance)

Congratulations. You have successfully defined the mechanics of your own rescue. You are ready for Part 6.

<u>My Statement of Faith (after part 5)</u>

PART 6 - THE HOLY SPIRIT: God With Us

In this part, we're exploring the Holy Spirit, not as a vague force, but as God's real presence with His people. We'll talk about new birth, how real change happens, how conviction and comfort work, and how to think wisely about guidance and spiritual gifts without getting weird or getting cynical. The goal is to help you write an "About the Holy Spirit" section that's biblical and balanced, and to give you a practical, grounded way to think about what it means to follow Jesus day to day with God's help, not just willpower.

Brick #24: New Birth and Indwelling

Cold Open Moment

Think about your last New Year's resolution.

You probably wrote down a bold list of things you were going to change. You were going to work out every day, stop eating junk food, and finally stop looking at your phone right before bed. For the first three days, your willpower was incredible. But by the second week of January, your willpower collapsed, and you were back to your exact same habits.

Willpower is a terrible engine for permanent change.

If you try to live the Christian life using only your own willpower, you will burn out by the second week. You cannot just try harder to be a good Christian. You need an entirely new engine. You need someone else living inside of you.

Big Idea

The Holy Spirit is the third Person of the Trinity who gives you a completely new spiritual life and personally lives inside you.

Why This Matters

This is the difference between dead religion and a living relationship.

If God only gave you the Bible and told you to follow the rules, you would be completely hopeless. It would be like a doctor giving a dead person a prescription and telling them to take their medicine.

- **You aren't fighting alone.** The power that raised Jesus from the dead is literally living inside your chest.
- **You are permanently marked.** The Holy Spirit's presence in your life is the ultimate proof that you belong to God.

Key Words

- **Holy Spirit:** The third Person of the Trinity. He is fully God, equal in power and glory with the Father and the Son.
- **Regeneration:** The supernatural act where God takes a spiritually dead heart and brings it to life (the "new birth").
- **Indwelling:** The reality that the Holy Spirit permanently lives inside every true believer.
- **Temple:** In the Old Testament, the building where God's presence lived; today, the believer's body is the temple of the Holy Spirit.

Precision Note (grown-up wording): Theologians clarify that the Holy Spirit is a divine *Person* (with a mind, will, and emotions), not just an impersonal *force* or energy.

Bible Receipts

Jesus tried to explain this "new engine" to a religious leader named Nicodemus.

Nicodemus had all the rules memorized, but Jesus told him it wasn't enough. "Truly I tell you, unless someone is born again, he cannot see the kingdom of God" (John 3:3, CSB). You don't need a makeover; you need a resurrection.

The prophet Ezekiel predicted exactly how this new birth would happen.

God promised, "I will give you a new heart and put a new spirit within you; I will remove your heart of stone and give you a heart of flesh. I will place my Spirit within you and cause you to follow my statutes and carefully observe my ordinances" (Ezekiel 36:26-27, CSB).

Notice the order. God doesn't say, "Follow the rules, and then I will give you my Spirit." He says, "I will put my Spirit inside you, and *He* will cause you to follow the rules." The Spirit isn't the reward for your obedience; He is the engine for it.

Truth in Plain English

First, you have to get the grammar right: The Holy Spirit is a "Who," not an "It."

He isn't a magical force field like the Force in Star Wars. He is God. He can be grieved. He can be lied to. He actively comforts, teaches, and prays for you.

Highlightable line: The Holy Spirit isn't just an emotion you feel during a worship song; He is the living God taking up residence in your life.

When you trust in Jesus, the Holy Spirit moves in. In the Old Testament, God's presence lived inside a massive stone building called the Temple. If you wanted to be near God, you had to travel to Jerusalem. But now, your physical body is the Temple. God doesn't live in a building anymore; He lives in you.

Common Confusion Box

Confusion #1: "I only get the Holy Spirit if I am a super spiritual Christian." This sounds right because we think God's presence is a reward for good behavior. But it's wrong. The Holy Spirit is not a VIP upgrade for elite Christians. Romans 8:9 (CSB) makes this terrifyingly clear: "If anyone does not have the Spirit of Christ, he does not belong to him." Every single true believer receives the Holy Spirit the exact moment they are saved.

Highlightable line: You do not need to beg for more of the Holy Spirit; the Holy Spirit simply needs more of you.

Confusion #2: "The Holy Spirit is the 'weird' part of the Trinity." This sounds right because you have probably seen viral clips of people doing bizarre, chaotic things in church and blaming it on the Holy Spirit. But here is what Scripture shows instead: The Holy Spirit is the Spirit of truth and order. Jesus said in John 16:14 that the primary job of the Holy Spirit is to glorify Jesus. If an action or a teaching draws massive attention to a human being instead of Jesus, the Holy Spirit is not the one doing it.

Why This Changes Real Life

When you grasp the reality of the indwelling Holy Spirit, you are never alone again.

When you walk into a crowded cafeteria where you feel completely invisible or judged for your faith, you are not walking in alone. The God of the universe is walking in with you. When you are sitting in your bedroom at 1:00 AM fighting a terrifying wave of anxiety, the Comforter is right there inside of you.

It also radically changes how you treat your own body.

If your body is just a shell, you can do whatever you want with it. But if your body is the actual Temple where the Holy Spirit lives, what you do with your eyes, your hands, and your sexuality becomes an act of worship. You honor your body because of the Guest who lives inside.

Try This This Week

The "Temple" Reminder. Sometime this week, when you feel incredibly weak or tempted to fall into an old habit, tap your chest twice with your hand. Say out loud: *"I am not empty. The Holy Spirit lives here."*

- Why do you think people are more comfortable talking about God the Father and Jesus than they are talking about the Holy Spirit?
- Read Ezekiel 36:26-27 again. Why is a "heart of stone" such a good description of a person before they know Jesus?
- How does realizing the Holy Spirit is a "Person" (who can be grieved or lied to) change the way you interact with Him?
- If your body is the Temple of the Holy Spirit, how should that change the way you view your physical health and your purity?

BELIEF BUILDER (Brick #24: About the Holy Spirit)

My one-sentence belief: "I believe the Holy Spirit is fully God, and He lives inside every believer to give us new life and the power to obey."

Bible receipts (pick 1–2): John 3:3; Ezekiel 36:26–27

This changes my life because: "I do not have to rely on my own weak willpower to live the Christian life."

One question I still have: (Write one honest question. No pretending.)

Short Prayer

Father, thank You for not leaving me alone to figure out this life. Jesus, thank You for sending the Comforter to live inside my heart. Holy Spirit, forgive me for treating You like a force instead of a Person. When I feel dead and empty, remind me of the new birth. Give me the power to honor the Temple You live in today. Amen.

My Notes & Thoughts

Brick #25: Growth: Fruit, Power, Conviction

Cold Open Moment

You know the sickening feeling in the pit of your stomach after you cross a line.

You say something incredibly harsh to your parents, or you cheat on a project, or you join in on tearing someone down in a group chat. Five minutes later, the adrenaline wears off, and a heavy, crushing weight sits on your chest.

How you interpret that heavy feeling will determine the entire trajectory of your faith.

If you think that weight is God telling you that you are worthless and He is done with you, you will run away and hide. But if you realize that weight is actually a surgical tool used by a loving God, you will run toward Him to be healed.

That heavy feeling isn't a sign that the Holy Spirit has abandoned you. It is the absolute proof that He is actively working on you.

Big Idea

The Holy Spirit actively grows us by convicting us of sin, giving us the power to fight it, and producing the fruit of His character in our lives.

Why This Matters

If you don't know how the Holy Spirit actually operates, you will constantly misread what God is doing in your life.

You will mistake conviction for condemnation, and you will mistake your own emotional highs for true spiritual growth.

- **It proves you belong to Him.** Unsaved people don't feel deep, spiritual grief over their sin; the fact that you feel convicted means you are alive.
- **It gives you the right metrics.** You measure your growth not by how many miracles you see, but by how much your character changes over time.

Key Words

- **Conviction:** The Holy Spirit graciously exposing your sin to your conscience so that you will repent and turn back to Jesus.
- **Condemnation:** The voice of the enemy telling you that your sin makes you worthless and permanently rejected by God.
- **Fruit of the Spirit:** The nine character traits (love, joy, peace, patience, kindness, goodness, faithfulness, gentleness,

self-control) that the Spirit naturally grows in a believer.

- **Illumination:** The Holy Spirit turning the "lights on" in your brain so you can actually understand the Bible when you read it.

Precision Note (grown-up wording): Theologians describe the Holy Spirit's ongoing work of changing our desires and actions as *synergistic*, meaning God's grace and our active effort are working together.

Bible Receipts

Jesus explained exactly what the Holy Spirit was going to do when He arrived on earth.

"When he comes, he will convict the world about sin, righteousness, and judgment" (John 16:8, CSB).

The Holy Spirit is the ultimate truth-teller. He refuses to let you stay comfortable in rebellion. He shines a blazing light on the darkest, ugliest parts of your heart, not to shame you, but to save you.

The Apostle Paul explains what happens when you actually yield to that conviction.

"But the fruit of the Spirit is love, joy, peace, patience, kindness, goodness, faithfulness, gentleness, and self-control. The law is not against such things" (Galatians 5:22-23, CSB).

Notice that Paul calls it *fruit*, not *results*. A factory produces results through grinding mechanical effort. An apple tree produces fruit simply by staying connected to its roots. You don't get the fruit of the Spirit by aggressively trying to be more patient; you get it by aggressively staying connected to Jesus.

Truth in Plain English

You have to learn the difference between conviction and condemnation.

Condemnation is a broad, heavy blanket. It whispers, "You are a terrible person. You are a fake. God is disgusted with you." It drives you away from God and into hiding. That is the voice of the enemy.

Conviction is a sharp, precise scalpel. It says, "What you said to your mom this morning was arrogant and cruel. You need to apologize." It drives you directly to the cross for forgiveness. That is the voice of the Holy Spirit.

Highlightable line: The enemy accuses you to destroy you; the Holy Spirit convicts you to rebuild you.

When you listen to the conviction of the Holy Spirit, He gives you the power to actually obey. You will start to notice that you have a supernatural patience you didn't have last year. You will have self-control in areas that used to dominate you.

Common Confusion Box

Confusion #1: "If I'm not feeling intense emotions during worship, the Holy Spirit isn't moving." This sounds right because we often equate the presence of God with goosebumps or tears. But it's wrong. The primary evidence of the Holy Spirit is not emotional hype; it is a holy life. You can cry through a three-hour worship set and still treat your siblings like garbage on the ride home. The truest mark of the Spirit's power is the slow, steady growth of His fruit in your everyday actions.

Highlightable line: The Holy Spirit isn't an emotional drug; He is a character architect.

Confusion #2: "I can't understand the Bible, so God must not be speaking to me." This sounds right because reading the Bible can feel incredibly dry and confusing. But here is what Scripture shows instead: The Holy Spirit is the author of the Bible, and He is also your personal tutor (1 Corinthians 2). If you open the Bible and ask the Holy Spirit for *illumination*, He will literally open your mind to understand what the text means.

Why This Changes Real Life

When you understand how the Holy Spirit works, you stop being crushed by your own failures.

When you inevitably mess up, you won't spiral into a depression. You will feel the sharp sting of conviction, and instead of hiding, you will immediately agree with God. You will say, "You are right. That was pride. I repent."

And it changes how you approach your own personal growth.

You don't have to wake up every day and manufacture your own joy or force yourself to be patient. You wake up, surrender your day to the Holy Spirit, and ask Him to produce His fruit through you. You stop relying on white-knuckle willpower and start relying on His endless power.

Try This This Week

The "Fruit Check." Look at the list in Galatians 5:22-23 (love, joy, peace, patience, kindness, goodness, faithfulness, gentleness, self-control). Pick the one trait you struggle with the most. Every morning this week, pray: *"Holy Spirit, I am completely out of [insert trait]. Please produce it in me today."*

Talk It Out

- Based on your own experience, how would you describe the difference between the feeling of condemnation and the feeling of conviction?
- Why is it so dangerous to measure your spiritual health by how emotional you feel during a church service?
- Read Galatians 5:22-23 again. Why do you think Paul calls these character traits "fruit" instead of "accomplishments"?
- How does the Holy Spirit's role of *illumination* change the way you should read your Bible?

BELIEF BUILDER (Brick #25: About the Holy Spirit)

My one-sentence belief: "I believe the Holy Spirit actively convicts me of sin, illuminates the Bible for me, and slowly produces the fruit of Christ's character in my life."

Bible receipts (pick 1–2): John 16:8; Galatians 5:22–23

This changes my life because: "I can learn to welcome God's conviction instead of hiding from it, knowing He is trying to heal me."

One question I still have: (Write one honest question. No pretending.)

Short Prayer

Father, thank You for loving me enough to not let me stay comfortable in my sin. Jesus, thank You for protecting me from condemnation. Holy Spirit, give me the wisdom to recognize Your sharp, loving conviction. Produce Your fruit in my life today. I want to look more like Jesus. Amen.

My Notes & Thoughts

Brick #26: Gifts and Guidance (with humility)

Cold Open Moment

You have to make a massive decision, and you have absolutely no idea what to do.

Maybe you are trying to decide which college to attend. Maybe you are wondering if you should break up with your boyfriend or girlfriend. Or maybe you are trying to figure out what career path to take. You know God has a plan, so you pray and ask Him to give you a sign.

You tell yourself, *If the next song on Spotify mentions a city, that's where I'll go to college.* Or, *If the traffic light turns green right now, it means God wants me to text them.*

We are absolutely desperate for the Holy Spirit to guide us, but we usually look for His guidance in the form of magic tricks, horoscopes, and random signs.

We treat the Holy Spirit like a cosmic Magic 8-Ball. But the Holy Spirit is much better than a fortune teller. He doesn't just want to micromanage your calendar; He wants to give you the wisdom to make good decisions, and the gifts to serve His church.

Big Idea

The Holy Spirit guides us primarily through Scripture and wisdom, and He gives every believer specific gifts to build up the church.

Why This Matters

If you don't understand how the Holy Spirit guides you, decision-making will paralyze you.

You will be terrified to pick a college or a career, constantly fearing that one wrong step will ruin God's "perfect plan" for your life.

- **It kills decision paralysis.** God steers moving ships. He gives you the freedom to make wise choices within the boundaries of His word.
- **It gives you a job.** You aren't just a spectator in the church; the Holy Spirit has given you specific tools to help build the Kingdom.

Key Words

- **Spiritual Gifts:** Supernatural abilities given by the Holy Spirit to every believer for the specific purpose of serving others.

- **Guidance:** The Holy Spirit directing your life, primarily by helping you apply the Bible to your specific situations.
- **Wisdom:** The God-given ability to look at a complex situation and make a choice that honors Jesus.
- **Edification:** Building up and encouraging other believers in their faith.

Precision Note (grown-up wording): Theologians distinguish between God's *Secret Will* (His sovereign plan for the future, which we don't know) and His *Revealed Will* (His commands in the Bible, which we are responsible to obey).

Bible Receipts

The Apostle Paul wanted the early church to know that every single person in the room mattered.

"A manifestation of the Spirit is given to each person for the common good" (1 Corinthians 12:7, CSB).

Notice two massive truths in that single verse. First, a gift is given to *each person*. If you are saved, you have a spiritual gift. You aren't benched. Second, the gift isn't for you. It is for the *common good*. Spiritual gifts are not merit badges to prove how holy you are; they are tools in a toolbox designed to build other people up.

But how does the Spirit guide us when we don't know what to do?

King David wrote, "Your word is a lamp for my feet and a light on my path" (Psalm 119:105, CSB).

The Holy Spirit is the author of the Bible. Therefore, the primary way the Holy Spirit will ever speak to you is through the book He already wrote. A lamp doesn't show you the destination ten miles down the road; it just gives you enough light to take the next faithful step.

Truth in Plain English

You do not have to live in terror of missing God's will.

God's will for your life is actually very simple: Be holy, love God, and love your neighbor. If you are doing those things, you are entirely free to choose which college you want to attend. You are free to pick your major.

Highlightable line: The Holy Spirit will never, ever lead you to do something that contradicts the Bible.

If you are dating someone who doesn't follow Jesus, you don't need to pray and ask for a sign if you should marry them. The Holy Spirit already wrote a book telling you not to be unequally yoked.

When you have a tough decision, the Holy Spirit guides you by giving you peace, aligning your desires with His, and speaking through the wise advice of mature Christians around you.

Faithful Christians Differ: Miraculous Gifts

You will likely encounter a debate within Christianity about the "miraculous" spiritual gifts (like speaking in tongues, prophecy, and miraculous healing).

Continuationists believe that all the spiritual gifts mentioned in the New Testament are still active today and should be eagerly desired by the church. **Cessationists** believe that the miraculous sign gifts were given specifically to the Apostles to establish the early church and write the New Testament, and they ceased (stopped) when the Bible was completed.

How to disagree well: Both sides agree that God still heals today, and both sides agree that the Bible is the ultimate authority. We must not mock Christians who experience the Holy Spirit differently than we do, and we must test every experience against the truth of Scripture.

Why This Changes Real Life

When you realize that the Holy Spirit has gifted you, you stop being a consumer at church.

A lot of teenagers show up to youth group, sit in the back row, critique the music, and complain that the message was boring. They treat church like a movie theater. But when you discover your spiritual gifts, church becomes a construction site.

Maybe you have the gift of encouragement, and your job is to seek out the lonely kids. Maybe you have the gift of leadership, teaching, or serving behind the scenes. You are desperately needed.

And when it comes to your future, you can finally exhale. You don't have to look for a secret message in your cereal bowl. You study the Bible, you seek wise advice, you pray for the Spirit's wisdom, and then you just step forward in confidence.

Highlightable line: God doesn't hide His will to trick you; He gives you His word to guide you.

Try This This Week

The "Next Step" Filter. If you are facing a confusing decision right now, don't ask for a random sign. Ask three questions: 1) Does this contradict the Bible? 2) What do the wisest Christians in my life think about it? 3) Does this choice make me look more like Jesus?

Talk It Out

- Why is it so tempting to ask God for a "random sign" instead of just doing the hard work of reading the Bible and seeking wisdom?
- Read 1 Corinthians 12:7 again. If spiritual gifts are meant for the "common good," what happens to a church when half the people don't use their gifts?
- Have you ever felt paralyzed trying to figure out "God's perfect plan" for your life? What helps break that paralysis?
- How does the Holy Spirit use the advice of older, wiser Christians to guide you?

BELIEF BUILDER (Brick #26: About the Holy Spirit)

My one-sentence belief: "I believe the Holy Spirit guides me primarily through the Bible and gives me specific spiritual gifts to serve the church."

Bible receipts (pick 1–2): 1 Corinthians 12:7; Psalm 119:105

This changes my life because: "I don't have to panic about my future; I can confidently take the next wise step in front of me."

One question I still have: (Write one honest question. No pretending.)

Short Prayer

Father, thank You for not leaving me in the dark. Jesus, thank You for trusting me with gifts to help build Your Kingdom. Holy Spirit, give me the wisdom to make good decisions today. Keep me from seeking magical signs instead of seeking Your word. Help me to use my life to build up the people around me. Amen.

<u>My Notes & Thoughts</u>

PART 6 - CHECKPOINT

Assemble Your Sixth Statement Section: "About the Holy Spirit"

You made it through Part 6. You just tackled the reality of the third Person of the Trinity. You looked at how He brings dead hearts to life, convicts us of sin, grows our character, and guides our decisions.

Now it is time to cement these three new bricks into the next section of your Personal Statement of Faith.

Step 1: Gather Your Bricks

Look back at the Belief Builder sections from Chapters 24, 25, and 26. Write your three one-sentence beliefs right here:

- **Brick 24 (New Birth & Indwelling):** ______________________________
- **Brick 25 (Growth & Conviction):** ______________________________
- **Brick 26 (Gifts & Guidance):** ______________________________

Step 2: Edit for Power

Look at the sentences you just wrote and apply the "**Red Pen Rules**":

1. **Assert His Personhood.** Make sure your paragraph refers to the Holy Spirit as "He" and not "It."
2. **Highlight His primary jobs.** Ensure you mention His role in saving us (new birth), growing us (fruit/conviction), and equipping us (gifts).
3. **Upgrade your vocabulary.** Circle and use your precision words: *indwells*, *convicts*, *illuminates*, *fruit*, and *spiritual gifts*.

Step 3: Draft Your Official Paragraph

Now, combine your edited bricks into one flowing paragraph. This is your confession about the power that lives inside of you.

My Statement of Faith: ABOUT THE HOLY SPIRIT

(Example Draft: "I believe the Holy Spirit is fully God, who brings spiritually dead hearts to life and permanently indwells every believer. He does not leave me alone, but actively convicts me of sin and slowly produces the fruit of Christ's character in my life. I believe He illuminates the Bible to guide my decisions, and He gives me specific spiritual gifts to serve and build up the church.")

Step 4: The 10-Second Spoken Test

If a friend asks you, "Who is the Holy Spirit anyway? Is He like a ghost?" you need to be able to answer quickly and confidently.

Look at your drafted paragraph and condense it into a single, spoken script.

My 10-Second Spoken Script:

"I believe the Holy Spirit is God living inside of me, giving me the power to fight sin, understand the Bible, and serve the church."

Read your 10-second script out loud right now. Practice it until you can say it without stumbling.

Step 5: Log Your Receipts

Pick the **three strongest Bible verses** from Part 6 that back up your new paragraph, and write the references here.

1. ________________________________ (Example: Ezekiel 36:26-27 - New Heart/Indwelling)
2. ________________________________ (Example: Galatians 5:22-23 - Fruit of the Spirit)
3. ________________________________ (Example: 1 Corinthians 12:7 - Spiritual Gifts)

Congratulations. You have successfully defined the power that fuels the Christian life. You are ready for Part 7.

<u>My Statement of Faith (after part 6)</u>

PART 7 - THE CHURCH: A FAMILY WITH A MISSION

In this part, we're talking about the church, what it is, what it isn't, and why you still need it even if you've seen hypocrisy. We'll explore worship as more than music, the meaning of baptism and the Lord's Supper (and why Christians sometimes disagree on details), and what it looks like to live on mission in a loud, complicated world. The goal is to help you write an "About the Church" section for your Statement of Faith that's honest and hopeful, and to see the church as God's plan for forming you, not just an event you attend.

Brick #27: What the Church Is (and isn't)

Cold Open Moment

You are sitting in a hard chair, staring at the back of someone's head, wondering why you have to be here.

The music is too loud (or too boring). The sermon feels like it is dragging on forever. You look around the room at the people, some of them are weird, some of them are annoying, and some of them are massive hypocrites.

You think to yourself, *I could just listen to a better sermon on a podcast. I could just worship God alone in the woods. Why do I have to go to a building to be a Christian?*

We live in a culture that treats church like a restaurant. If we don't like the food, the service, or the vibe, we just leave a one-star review in our heads and go find a different one. Or we stop going entirely.

But if you treat the church like a business, you will completely miss the beauty of what God actually built. Jesus didn't die to start a religious country club. He died to build a family.

Big Idea

The church isn't a building you go to or an event you watch; it is the living, breathing family of God that you belong to.

Why This Matters

If you misunderstand the church, you will try to live the Christian life completely alone, and you will not survive it.

- **It kills consumer Christianity.** You stop evaluating your youth group based on how much it entertains you, and you start looking for ways you can serve.
- **It gives you a safety net.** When your faith feels weak and you can't carry your own burdens, your spiritual family carries them for you.

Key Words

- **Church (Ekklesia):** The Greek word used in the New Testament, meaning "a gathered assembly of called out people."
- **Universal Church:** Every single true believer in Jesus across all of history and around the entire globe.
- **Local Church:** A specific group of believers in a specific city who gather together regularly to worship and serve.
- **Body of Christ:** The biblical metaphor showing that every Christian is a connected, vital body part under the

headship of Jesus.

Precision Note (grown-up wording): Theologians distinguish between the *visible church* (everyone who attends a church building) and the *invisible church* (only the people who are truly saved and known by God).

Bible Receipts

The Apostle Peter wanted the early Christians to know exactly who they were. They were facing intense persecution, and they felt incredibly small.

Peter writes, "But you are a chosen race, a royal priesthood, a holy nation, a people for his possession, so that you may proclaim the praises of the one who called you out of darkness into his marvelous light" (1 Peter 2:9, CSB).

You are a holy nation. A people. God doesn't just save individuals and put them in isolated jars; He saves individuals and immediately fuses them together into a new family.

The Apostle Paul uses the human body to explain how this actually works.

"Now you are the body of Christ, and individual members of it" (1 Corinthians 12:27, CSB). Just a few verses earlier, Paul says that the eye cannot say to the hand, "I don't need you!"

If you cut a hand off a body, the hand doesn't become an "independent hand." It dies. A Christian who completely disconnects from the local church is like a severed hand trying to survive on its own.

Truth in Plain English

You cannot love Jesus and hate His bride.

The Bible repeatedly calls the church the "Bride of Christ." If someone walked up to you and said, "I think you are awesome, but I absolutely despise your wife," you wouldn't be friends with that person. Jesus feels the exact same way about His church.

Highlightable line: The church isn't an event you attend on Sunday; it is an identity you live out on Monday.

Is the church messy? Absolutely. It is full of broken, selfish, flawed human beings. But that is the entire point. The church is not a museum for perfect people to show off their flawless lives. It is a hospital for sick people who are all relying on the exact same cure.

Common Confusion Box

Confusion #1: "I can be a good Christian without going to church." This sounds right because your salvation is based on your personal faith in Jesus, not your church attendance record. But it's wrong. While going to church doesn't *save* you, the New Testament knows absolutely nothing about a "solo Christian." The Bible contains dozens of "one another" commands (love one another, bear one another's burdens, forgive one another). You cannot obey the commands of Jesus if you are sitting alone in your bedroom.

Highlightable line: A Christian without a church is like a football player without a team; you might have the uniform, but you aren't actually in the game.

Confusion #2: "The church is full of hypocrites." This sounds right because every single one of us has been hurt or disappointed by someone in the church who said one thing and did another. But here is what Scripture shows instead: The church has never claimed to be full of perfect people. 1 John 1:8 says that if we claim to be without sin, we are liars. Yes, there are hypocrites in the church, just like there are hypocrites at your school and in your own mirror. We don't gather because we are perfect; we gather because Jesus is.

Why This Changes Real Life

When you change your view of the church from a "restaurant" to a "family," your entire Sunday morning experience flips upside down.

When you walk into a restaurant, you expect to be served. If the food is cold, you complain. But when you walk into your own kitchen at home, you don't expect to be served. You help set the table. You help do the dishes.

You belong there.

If you are a Christian, the church is your kitchen. You don't get to just sit in the back row with your arms crossed, waiting for the youth pastor to entertain you. You have a job to do. You are called to encourage the younger kids, pray for your friends, and help carry the weight of the ministry.

Try This This Week

The "Not a Consumer" Challenge. This Sunday at church or youth group, intentionally look for one person who is sitting alone or looks uncomfortable. Walk up to them, ask them their name, and have a two-minute conversation. Stop consuming and start building the family.

Talk It Out

- Why do you think so many people treat church like a consumer product (leaving a "bad review" if they don't like the music or the sermon)?
- Read 1 Corinthians 12:27 again. How does the metaphor of a human body completely destroy the idea of "solo Christianity"?
- Have you ever been hurt by someone in the church? How can we acknowledge that pain without abandoning the church entirely?

BELIEF BUILDER (Brick #27: About the Church)

My one-sentence belief: "I believe the church is not a building, but the living family of God, and I am called to be an active, connected member of it."

Bible receipts (pick 1–2): 1 Peter 2:9; 1 Corinthians 12:27

This changes my life because: "I can stop treating church like a consumer and start serving the people around me like family."

One question I still have: (Write one honest question. No pretending.)

Short Prayer

Father, thank You for adopting me into a massive, worldwide family. Jesus, forgive me for the times I have criticized Your beautiful, messy bride. Holy Spirit, give me a deep love for the people in my local church. Help me to stop being a consumer who only wants to be entertained. Show me how to serve my spiritual family this week. Amen.

My Notes & Thoughts

Brick #28: Worship: More Than Music

Cold Open Moment

The lights go down in the sanctuary. The band starts playing the opening chords of a really popular song. The youth pastor tells everyone to stand up.

You look to your left, and someone has their hands raised in the air, eyes closed, looking incredibly emotional. You look to your right, and someone is passionately singing every single word.

Then you look at yourself. You don't feel anything.

Your heart isn't beating faster. You don't have tears in your eyes. You are just standing there, awkwardly holding your phone, wondering what you are going to eat for lunch. And a wave of guilt washes over you. *Is my worship broken? Why don't I feel God like everyone else does?*

We have bought into a massive lie about what worship actually is. We have reduced "worship" to a 20-minute musical set on Sunday morning, and we have tied it completely to our emotional hype. But biblical worship is infinitely bigger than music.

Big Idea

Worship isn't just singing a slow song on Sunday; it is the act of offering your entire, everyday life to God for His glory.

Why This Matters

If you limit worship to music, you will completely compartmentalize your faith.

You will be a "Christian" on Sunday morning, but an atheist on Tuesday afternoon when you are doing your homework or playing a sport.

- **It validates your boring days.** When you understand true worship, taking out the trash and taking a math test can actually become holy moments.
- **It takes the pressure off.** You don't have to manufacture fake emotions during the music set to please God.

Key Words

- **Worship:** To assign ultimate worth, honor, and priority to God above everything else in your life.
- **Glorify:** To make God look as big, beautiful, and important as He actually is.
- **Idolatry:** Giving your highest worship, love, or obedience to anything other than God.

- **Sacrifice:** Giving up something valuable (like your time, money, or comfort) to honor God.

Precision Note (grown-up wording): Theologians state that the chief end of man is to *glorify God and enjoy Him forever*; worship is the natural response of the creature to the Creator's infinite worth.

Bible Receipts

The Apostle Paul completely shatters our modern, music-only definition of worship in his letter to the Romans.

He writes, "Therefore, brothers and sisters, in view of the mercies of God, I urge you to present your bodies as a living sacrifice, holy and pleasing to God; this is your true worship" (Romans 12:1, CSB).

Paul doesn't say, "Present your vocal cords for three songs." He says present your *bodies*. Your hands, your feet, your brain, your sexuality, your money. How you live your physical life is your true, spiritual worship.

But does music still matter? Absolutely.

The book of Psalms commands us: "Come, let us shout joyfully to the LORD, shout triumphantly to the rock of our salvation! Let us enter his presence with thanksgiving; let us shout triumphantly to him in song" (Psalm 95:1-2, CSB).

Music is a powerful, biblical tool that God gave us to focus our minds and stir our affections for Him. Music is a *form* of worship, but obedience is the *heart* of worship.

Truth in Plain English

Every single human being on the planet is a worshipper.

You cannot turn your worship engine off. You are always assigning ultimate value to something. If it isn't God, it will be your grades, your athletic performance, your romantic relationship, or your follower count.

Whatever you worship will control you. If you worship your grades, a failed test will completely destroy your identity. If you worship a relationship, a breakup will make you feel like your life is over.

Highlightable line: Only God is big enough to handle the crushing weight of your worship without breaking your heart.

When you sing at church, you are just realigning your worship engine. You are using the lyrics to remind your forgetful brain that Jesus is the only one actually worthy of the throne in your life.

Common Confusion Box

Confusion #1: "I can't worship if I don't like the style of the song." This sounds right because we live in a consumer culture where we tailor every Spotify playlist to our exact personal preferences. But it's wrong. Worship is not about your preference; it is about God's worth. If the lyrics of the song are declaring the truth about who God is, you can worship Him, even if the drums are too loud or the melody is outdated. You aren't evaluating a concert; you are bringing an offering.

Highlightable line: Worship is not an emotional experience God provides for you; it is a sacrifice of praise you provide for Him.

Confusion #2: "If I don't feel emotional, my worship doesn't count." This sounds right because we often confuse the Holy Spirit with adrenaline. But here is what Scripture shows instead: Sometimes, the deepest act of worship is choosing to sing the truth about God's goodness while you are feeling entirely numb, depressed, or angry. Choosing to trust God when your emotions are dead is a massive, beautiful sacrifice.

Why This Changes Real Life

When you expand your definition of worship, your entire week lights up with purpose.

Right now, a lot of your life probably feels like meaningless busywork. You wake up, go to school, do homework, do chores, and go to bed. But Romans 12:1 changes all of that.

If you are writing a history paper, and you choose to work hard on it without cheating to honor God with your mind, that history paper is an act of worship. If your mom asks you to clean the kitchen, and you do it without complaining because you want to honor the authority God gave her, doing the dishes is an act of worship.

You don't have to wait for Sunday to connect with God. Every single ordinary moment is an opportunity to push back against idolatry and declare that Jesus is King.

Try This This Week

The "Ordinary Worship" Moment. Pick one incredibly boring or annoying task you have to do this week (like folding laundry, studying for a quiz, or cleaning your room). Before you start, pray out loud: *"God, I am doing this specific task as an act of worship to You today."*

Talk It Out

- Why do you think modern church culture has reduced the massive concept of "worship" to just the music part of a service?
- Read Romans 12:1 again. What does it actually look like in high school to present your body as a "living sacrifice"?
- Think about the idea that everyone worships something. What are the most common "idols" that teenagers worship today?
- How does realizing that your homework and your chores can be acts of worship change the way you view your daily schedule?

BELIEF BUILDER (Brick #28: About the Church/Christian Life)

My one-sentence belief: "I believe worship is more than just singing songs; it is offering my entire, everyday life to God for His glory."

Bible receipts (pick 1–2): Romans 12:1; Psalm 95:1–2

This changes my life because: "I can honor God on a random Tuesday afternoon just as much as I can on a Sunday morning."

One question I still have: (Write one honest question. No pretending.)

Short Prayer

Father, thank You for being infinitely worthy of all my love and attention. Jesus, forgive me for the times I have worshipped my own image, my grades, or my relationships instead of You. Holy Spirit, expand my view of worship. Help me to offer my daily chores, my homework, and my conversations as a living sacrifice. Amen.

My Notes & Thoughts

Brick #29: Baptism and the Lord's Supper

Cold Open Moment

If an alien landed on earth and walked into a church on a Sunday morning, they would probably be deeply confused.

They would watch an adult push a teenager backward into a giant tank of water while everyone cheered. Then, they would watch everyone in the room pass around tiny, cracker-like pieces of bread and microscopic cups of juice, eating them with serious looks on their faces.

To an outsider, our rituals look bizarre. And if you have grown up in the church, you have probably seen these things happen so many times that you don't even think about them anymore. You just wait for the water to stop splashing or for the juice cups to get passed down your row.

But Jesus didn't give us these practices just so we would have something to do to pass the time. He gave them to us because He knows how incredibly forgetful we are.

Big Idea

Baptism and the Lord's Supper are physical signs Jesus gave the church to constantly remind us of His invisible grace.

Why This Matters

We are physical creatures. We easily forget spiritual truths when our emotions get chaotic.

When you feel disconnected from God, or when your faith feels entirely theoretical, you need something you can actually touch, taste, and see to anchor you back to reality.

- **They are physical anchors.** They prove that Christianity isn't just a mental philosophy; it is based on blood, water, and real history.
- **They unite the family.** You are doing the exact same practices that Christians have been doing for 2,000 years all over the globe.

Key Words

- **Ordinance (or Sacrament):** A sacred, physical practice commanded by Jesus for His church to observe.
- **Baptism:** The act of being washed in water to publicly declare your faith in Jesus and your new life in Him.
- **The Lord's Supper (Communion):** A shared meal of bread and the cup to remember the broken body and spilled blood of Jesus on the cross.

- **Covenant:** A binding, unbreakable promise made by God to His people.

Precision Note (grown-up wording): Theologians often describe these ordinances as *visible words*, they physically preach the gospel of Jesus' death and resurrection without making a sound.

Bible Receipts

Jesus didn't make baptism optional. Before He ascended to heaven, He gave His followers their final marching orders.

"Go, therefore, and make disciples of all nations, baptizing them in the name of the Father and of the Son and of the Holy Spirit" (Matthew 28:19, CSB). Baptism is the universal initiation rite. It is the public badge that says, "I belong to the Triune God."

And on the night before He was crucified, Jesus established the Lord's Supper with His closest friends.

"For I received from the Lord what I also passed on to you: On the night when he was betrayed, the Lord Jesus took bread, and when he had given thanks, broke it, and said, 'This is my body, which is for you. Do this in remembrance of me'" (1 Corinthians 11:23-24, CSB).

Jesus knew that thousands of years later, we would struggle with doubt. So He attached His massive promise of forgiveness to everyday physical objects: bread and a cup.

Truth in Plain English

Think about baptism and communion like a wedding ring.

If someone puts a wedding ring on their finger, the metal doesn't magically make them married. The marriage happened when they made a covenant promise. But the ring is a visible, permanent symbol to the entire world that they belong to someone else.

Highlightable line: Getting baptized doesn't wash away your sins; it is the public announcement that Jesus' blood has already washed them away.

When you go under the water, you are physically acting out the gospel. You are saying, "My old, rebellious self died and was buried with Jesus." When you come up out of the water, you are saying, "I have been raised to a brand new life."

And the Lord's Supper is the family meal. When you chew the bread and taste the juice, you are physically reminding your forgetful brain that Jesus' body was actually crushed, and His blood was actually spilled for you.

Faithful Christians Differ: Baptism & Communion

You will likely see different churches practice these signs in different ways.

Baptism: Some Christians (like Baptists and non-denominational churches) believe baptism is only for people old enough to make their own decision (*Believer's Baptism*). Other faithful Christians (like Presbyterians, Anglicans, and Lutherans) baptize infants to welcome them into the covenant community.

Communion: Some churches believe the bread and cup are purely symbolic. Other churches believe Jesus is uniquely, spiritually present in the meal.

How to disagree well: We do not have to divide over this. We can worship together, knowing that both sides are trying their absolute best to honor exactly what the Bible commands.

Common Confusion Box

Confusion #1: "I shouldn't get baptized until I stop struggling with my sin." This sounds right because we think baptism is a graduation ceremony for perfect Christians. But it's wrong. Baptism isn't a trophy for flawless performance; it is a starting line for broken people. If you wait until you are perfect to get baptized, you will never get in the water. You don't get baptized to prove you are clean; you get baptized to declare that you need Jesus to clean you.

Highlightable line: The Lord's Supper isn't a meal for the perfect; it is medicine for the sick.

Confusion #2: "Taking communion is just a boring routine." This sounds right because we do it so often, and the elements (a tiny cracker) aren't very exciting. But here is what Scripture shows instead: 1 Corinthians 11 says that whenever we eat the bread and drink the cup, we "proclaim the Lord's death until he comes." It is a heavy, joyful, supernatural moment of remembering our rescue. If it feels boring, the problem is our attention span, not the meal.

Why This Changes Real Life

These physical signs are the ultimate antidote to spiritual anxiety.

When you are lying in bed, feeling entirely disconnected from God, your brain will try to convince you that your faith was just an emotional phase. But you can look back at a specific moment in time and space.

You can say, "No. On that specific Sunday, I physically went under the water. I publicly declared my allegiance to the King."

And every time you take the Lord's Supper, you are resetting your identity. You are holding the physical proof that your massive debt of sin was paid for in blood. You don't have to live in your head; God gave you something to hold in your hands.

Try This This Week

The "Next Communion" Commitment. The next time your church passes the elements for the Lord's Supper, do not eat the bread mindlessly. Hold it in your hand for ten seconds. Pray silently: *"Jesus, this represents the actual, physical body You allowed to be broken for me. Thank You."* ### Talk It Out

- If an outsider asked you why your church dunks people in water, how would you explain baptism in your own words?
- Read 1 Corinthians 11:23-24 again. Why do you think Jesus chose ordinary things like bread and a cup to help us remember Him?
- Look at the "Common Confusion" box. Why is it so dangerous to think you need to be "perfect" before getting baptized or taking communion?
- How does the wedding ring analogy help explain the difference between being saved and being baptized?

BELIEF BUILDER (Brick #29: About the Church)

My one-sentence belief: "I believe Jesus gave the church the physical signs of Baptism and the Lord's Supper to publicly declare and constantly remind us of His saving grace."

Bible receipts (pick 1–2): Matthew 28:19; 1 Corinthians 11:23–24

This changes my life because: "When my faith feels invisible and weak, God gives me tangible, physical reminders of His love to anchor me."

One question I still have: (Write one honest question. No pretending.)

Short Prayer

Father, thank You for knowing that I am weak and forgetful. Jesus, thank You for allowing Your body to be broken and Your blood to be spilled for my freedom. Holy Spirit, when I witness a baptism or take communion, fill me with a deep sense of awe. Keep these beautiful gifts from ever becoming boring routines in my mind. Amen.

My Notes & Thoughts

Brick #30: Mission and Witness (truth + love)

Cold Open Moment

The word "evangelism" probably makes you want to hide under your bed.

When you hear that you are supposed to share your faith, a very specific, terrifying image pops into your head. You picture yourself standing on a street corner holding a giant sign, or knocking on a stranger's door to ask them if they want to go to heaven, or getting into a brutal, screaming debate with an atheist in the comments section of a YouTube video.

You think to yourself, *I don't know all the answers. What if they ask me a question about dinosaurs or science that I don't know? What if they make fun of me? I'll just keep my faith to myself.*

But keeping your faith to yourself isn't actually an option if you follow Jesus.

The church is not a country club designed to keep Christians comfortable and safe from the outside world. The church is a rescue boat, and you have been handed a life jacket. If you know the cure to the disease, keeping quiet is the most unloving thing you could possibly do.

Big Idea

Being a witness simply means telling the truth about what Jesus has done for you, and doing it with massive amounts of love and respect.

Why This Matters

If you misunderstand your mission, you will live a completely self-centered Christian life.

You will go to church, listen to the music, read your Bible, and go to heaven, but you will leave a trail of spiritually dead friends behind you because you were too scared to speak up.

- **It takes the pressure off.** You aren't responsible for saving anyone; you are only responsible for sharing the truth.
- **It gives your life massive purpose.** Your high school is not just a place you endure for four years; it is your specific mission field.

Key Words

- **Evangelism:** The act of clearly sharing the good news (the gospel) of Jesus Christ with someone who doesn't know Him.
- **Witness:** Someone who simply testifies to what they have personally seen, heard, and experienced.

- **Mission:** The ongoing work of the church to push back the darkness and bring the light of the gospel to the entire world.

- **Apologetics:** The practice of giving a reasoned, logical defense for the truth of the Christian faith.

Precision Note (grown-up wording): Theologians talk about the *Great Commission*, which is Jesus' final command to His church to go into all the world, preach the gospel, and make disciples.

Bible Receipts

Jesus didn't give His followers a suggestion; He gave them a mandate.

Right before He ascended to heaven, He told them, "But you will receive power when the Holy Spirit has come on you, and you will be my witnesses in Jerusalem, in all Judea and Samaria, and to the ends of the earth" (Acts 1:8, CSB).

Notice the word He uses. *Witnesses*. A witness in a courtroom doesn't have to be a brilliant lawyer. They don't have to know every detail of the penal code. A witness just sits on the stand and says, "This is what I saw. This is what happened to me."

But how are we supposed to share this truth? The Apostle Peter gives us the rules of engagement.

"But in your hearts regard Christ the Lord as holy, ready at any time to give a defense to anyone who asks you for a reason for the hope that is in you. Yet do this with gentleness and respect..." (1 Peter 3:15-16, CSB).

You have to give a defense (the truth), but you must do it with gentleness and respect (love). Truth without love makes you a jerk. Love without truth makes you a liar.

Truth in Plain English

Evangelism is just one beggar telling another beggar where to find food.

You don't have to be a seminary professor to share your faith. If you know you are a sinner, and you know Jesus saved you by grace, you have enough theology to be a witness.

Highlightable line: You don't have to win an argument to win a soul.

The best way to share your faith isn't by screaming at people; it is by living a life that is so noticeably full of joy, peace, and grace that people actually ask you why you are different. And when they ask, you don't panic. You just point to Jesus.

If they ask a hard question that you don't know the answer to, the best thing you can say is, "That is an awesome question. I don't know the answer right now, but let me research it and get back to you." That kind of honesty builds massive trust.

Common Confusion Box

Confusion #1: "I will just preach the gospel through my actions; I don't need to use words." This sounds right because living a holy, loving life is incredibly important, and nobody likes a hypocrite. But it's wrong. Your good actions are the *setup*, but words are the *gospel*. The gospel literally means "good news." News cannot be acted out; it has to be spoken. If you live a great life but never mention Jesus, people will just assume you are a really nice, morally superior person, and God gets zero glory.

Highlightable line: Your actions give you the credibility to speak, but your words actually deliver the message of salvation.

Confusion #2: "If my friend rejects the gospel, I failed." This sounds right because we live in a results-oriented world. If we don't close the sale, we failed. But here is what Scripture shows instead: You do not have the power to change a human heart. Only the Holy Spirit can do that. In 1 Corinthians 3, Paul says that one person plants the seed, another waters it, but *God* makes it grow. Your job is just to plant the seed. God handles the harvest.

Why This Changes Real Life

When you grasp your identity as a witness, your everyday life becomes a high-stakes adventure.

You stop viewing your annoying coworker, your difficult lab partner, or your unbelieving coach as an inconvenience. You start viewing them as eternal souls who desperately need the exact same rescue you received.

It also cures your fear of rejection. If a friend makes fun of you for believing in Jesus, it stings, but it doesn't crush you. You know that Jesus was mocked, beaten, and killed for bringing the truth, so you shouldn't be surprised when you face a little bit of awkwardness in the cafeteria.

Highlightable line: The temporary awkwardness of sharing your faith is nothing compared to the eternal tragedy of staying silent.

Try This This Week

The "One Name" Prayer. Write down the first name of one friend or family member who does not know Jesus. Put that name on a sticky note on your mirror. Commit to praying for their salvation every single morning for the next seven days, and ask God to give you one natural opportunity to talk about your faith with them.

Talk It Out

- When you hear the word "evangelism," what is the first image or emotion that pops into your head? Why?
- Read 1 Peter 3:15-16 again. Why is it so incredibly damaging to the church when Christians share the truth, but do it without "gentleness and respect"?
- Why is it actually a massive relief to realize that you cannot save anyone, and that only the Holy Spirit can change a heart?

BELIEF BUILDER (Brick #30: About the Church)

My one-sentence belief: "I believe the church is on a mission, and I am called to be a witness, sharing the gospel of Jesus with truth, gentleness, and respect."

Bible receipts (pick 1–2): Acts 1:8; 1 Peter 3:15

This changes my life because: "I can boldly share what Jesus has done for me without carrying the pressure of having to save anyone."

One question I still have: (Write one honest question. No pretending.)

Short Prayer

Father, thank You for trusting me with the greatest news in the universe. Jesus, forgive me for the times I have stayed silent because I was afraid of looking foolish. Holy Spirit, give me the boldness to speak the truth and the gentleness to do it with love. Open the hearts of my friends who don't know You yet. Use my ordinary life to point people to Your extraordinary grace. Amen.

My Notes & Thoughts

PART 7 - CHECKPOINT

Assemble Your Seventh Statement Section: "About the Church"

You made it through Part 7. You just moved from personal theology to family theology. You defined what the church actually is, what it means to truly worship, why we have physical signs like baptism, and what our mission is in the world.

It is time to cement these four new bricks into the next section of your Personal Statement of Faith.

Step 1: Gather Your Bricks

Look back at the Belief Builder sections from Chapters 27 through 30. Write your four one-sentence beliefs right here:

- **Brick 27 (What the Church Is):** ____
- **Brick 28 (Worship):** ____
- **Brick 29 (Baptism & Communion):** ____
- **Brick 30 (Mission & Witness):** ____

Step 2: Edit for Power

Look at the sentences you just wrote. You are assembling the doctrine of the church, so you want it to sound communal. Apply the **"Red Pen Rules"**:

1. **Use plural language.** Instead of saying "I go to church," try shifting the tone to "The church is the family of God."
2. **Connect the practices.** Group your sentence about worship and your sentence about the ordinances (baptism/communion) together, as they are both ways the church responds to God.
3. **Upgrade your vocabulary.** Circle and use your precision words: *Body of Christ*, *living sacrifice*, *ordinances*, and *gospel*.

Step 3: Draft Your Official Paragraph

Now, combine your edited bricks into one flowing paragraph. This is your confession about the family you belong to.

My Statement of Faith: ABOUT THE CHURCH

(Example Draft: "I believe the church is the living Body of Christ and the family of God, not just a building or an event. As a connected member, I am called to live a life of everyday worship, offering myself as a living sacrifice. I believe Jesus gave the church the ordinances of Baptism and the Lord's Supper as physical signs to publicly declare and remember His saving grace. The church is on a mission, and I am called to be a faithful witness, sharing the gospel with truth and love.")

Step 4: The 10-Second Spoken Test

If a friend says, "I love Jesus, I just don't like organized religion or the church," you need to be able to explain why the church isn't optional.

Look at your drafted paragraph and condense it into a single, spoken script.

My 10-Second Spoken Script:

"I believe the church is the family of God, given signs to remember His grace, and called to a mission to share His truth with the world."

Read your 10-second script out loud right now. Practice it until you can say it with conviction.

Step 5: Log Your Receipts

Pick the **three strongest Bible verses** from Part 7 that back up your new paragraph, and write the references here.

1. ______________________________ (Example: 1 Corinthians 12:27 - Body of Christ)
2. ______________________________ (Example: Romans 12:1 - Worship)
3. ______________________________ (Example: 1 Peter 3:15 - Mission/Defense)

Congratulations. You have successfully defined your spiritual family and your earthly mission. You are ready for Part 8.

<u>My Statement of Faith (after part 7)</u>

PART 8 - THE CHRISTIAN LIFE: WISDOM, SUFFERING, HOLINESS

In this part, we're getting practical about following Jesus when it's hard. We'll talk about what discipleship looks like under pressure, what to do with suffering, how to make decisions without fear, and how real growth happens over time. The goal isn't perfection, it's direction. By the end, you'll be able to write an "About the Christian Life" section that's realistic, hopeful, and usable, and you'll have a few anchors you can return to when temptation, anxiety, or disappointment tries to take over.

Brick #31: Following Jesus When It Costs You

Cold Open Moment

The notification pings at 11:15 PM. You look at your glowing screen in the dark, and your stomach immediately drops. It's the group chat. Your friends are absolutely tearing into someone who isn't there, sharing screenshots, making jokes, and escalating the cruelty by the minute.

You know it's wrong. You know this person is being destroyed behind their back.

But you also know the unspoken rule of this group: if you defend the target, you become the next target. If you type, "Hey guys, this is messed up, let's stop," you risk being kicked out, mocked, and sitting alone at lunch tomorrow. The easiest thing in the world is to just send a laughing emoji and go to sleep. It costs you nothing right now.

But doing the right thing? Speaking up? Stepping away? That is going to cost you. It might cost you your reputation, your comfort, or your closest friend group. Welcome to the hardest part of the Christian life.

Big Idea

Following Jesus is a completely free gift that will cost you everything you used to rely on, and it is entirely worth it.

Why This Matters

If you think following God is just a life-hack to make everything easier, you are going to panic and quit the second things get hard. But if you understand the cost upfront, you won't be surprised. Knowing the cost matters because:

- It protects you from feeling like God abandoned you when life gets difficult.
- It proves your faith is actually real, not just a phase.
- It opens your eyes to the massive reward that makes the cost look tiny in comparison.

Key Words

Cost of Discipleship: The things you willingly give up, like comfort, popularity, or control over your own life, in order to follow Jesus. *Precision Note: This phrase was popularized by theologian Dietrich Bonhoeffer, contrasting "costly grace" (which demands our whole life) against "cheap grace" (which asks for nothing).*

Holiness: Being set apart and looking distinctly different from the world around you because you are reflecting the character of Jesus. *Precision Note: Derived from the Hebrew root word qadosh, meaning to be separated, cut off, or dedicated to a sacred purpose.*

Idolatry: Treating a good thing (like your friendships, your grades, or your reputation) as an ultimate thing that you can't live without. *Precision Note: The primary sin addressed throughout Scripture; it is the act of replacing the Creator with creation as the source of human identity and security.*

Bible Receipts

Luke 9:23–24 *"If anyone wants to follow after me, let him deny himself, take up his cross daily, and follow me. For whoever wants to save his life will lose it, but whoever loses his life because of me will save it."* When Jesus said "take up your cross," He wasn't talking about wearing a piece of jewelry. To a first-century teenager, a cross was a horrific execution device. Jesus was bluntly saying that following Him means putting your own selfish agenda to death. You don't get to be in the driver's seat of your life anymore.

Matthew 13:44 *"The kingdom of heaven is like treasure, buried in a field, that a man found and reburied. Then in his joy he goes and sells everything he has and buys that field."* Notice the emotion here. The man sells literally everything he owns, but he isn't sad about it. He does it "in his joy." Why? Because what he is gaining is infinitely more valuable than the junk he is giving up.

Truth in Plain English

A lot of people want Jesus to be a hobby. They want to add Him to their life like a new extracurricular activity, right alongside soccer, band, and video games.

But Jesus doesn't do hobbies. He demands a complete takeover.

Grace is entirely free. You cannot earn your salvation, and you don't have to clean yourself up before God accepts you. But once you are adopted into His family, the way you live changes. **Grace is entirely free, but following Jesus will cost you your pride, your comfort, and your right to run your own life.**

This means you will have to say "no" to your own desires sometimes. It means you might have to break off a dating relationship because it's pulling you away from God. It means you might have to confess a secret you've been hiding, even though the embarrassment feels unbearable.

Jesus doesn't just want your Sunday mornings; He wants your group chats, your browser history, and your weekend plans. When you start living like that, the world is going to look at you funny. People might call you extreme, judgmental, or boring. That hurts. No one likes being misunderstood. But the secret to the Christian life is realizing that the reward is better than the sacrifice. **You can survive losing the approval of the crowd when you already have the approval of the King.** ### Common Confusion Box **What people think:** If I give my life to God, He will protect me from missing out, losing friends, or going through hard times. **Why it sounds right:** God loves us, right? And love means wanting people to be happy and comfortable. **Why it's wrong:** God's ultimate goal isn't your temporary, daily comfort. His goal is your eternal joy and your holiness. Sometimes, our "comfort" is the exact thing keeping us from trusting Him. If God never let you lose anything, you would never learn that He is all you actually need. **What Scripture shows instead:** Jesus made a bold promise in John 16:33: "In this world you will have trouble." But He didn't stop there. He followed it up with: "But take heart! I have overcome the world."

Why This Changes Real Life

Let's get really practical. Think about the Fear Of Missing Out (FOMO). It is a suffocating anxiety. You see the pictures of the hangout you weren't invited to. You hear the stories about the party you walked away from because things were getting out of hand.

When you choose Jesus over the crowd, there is a very real sting. It feels lonely. It feels like you are paying a massive tax that nobody else has to pay.

But knowing the cost changes how you process that pain. When you get mocked for holding onto your purity, or when you lose a friend because you refuse to cheat on a massive history final, you don't have to spiral into despair. You can actually expect it.

You start to realize that the things you are losing were never going to last anyway. High school popularity fades incredibly fast. The approval of people who want you to compromise your character isn't worth keeping.

When you embrace the cost of following Jesus, it actually makes you fearless. If your identity isn't built on what other teenagers think of you, then other teenagers can't destroy your identity. You become unshakeable.

Try This This Week

Identify one specific area where following Jesus feels costly to you right now. It might be a habit you need to drop, a friend you need to set a boundary with, or a media choice you need to cut out. Write it down on a piece of paper. Pray over it, explicitly telling God it hurts to let it go, but ask Him for the strength to choose Him anyway. Then, rip the paper up and throw it away.

Talk It Out

- **Easy:** What is honestly the hardest thing about being a Christian at your school or in your friend group?
- **Real:** Have you ever compromised what you believe or stayed silent just to fit in? (No shame, we all have. What happened?)
- **Hard:** If someone looked at how you spend your free time and your money, would they be able to tell that Jesus is your ultimate treasure?
- **Group-Friendly:** What is one specific way we can support each other this week when doing the right thing feels lonely?

BELIEF BUILDER

(Write these down in your notes, this is your brick for this chapter!)

- **My one-sentence belief:** "I believe following Jesus means giving up my right to run my own life, but He is a treasure worth any cost."
- **Bible receipts:** Luke 9:23; Matthew 13:44.
- **This changes my life because:** It gives me the courage to stand alone when I have to, knowing I am never actually alone.
- **One question I still have:** How do I know when to speak up boldly and when to just walk away quietly?

Short Prayer

Jesus, following You is honestly harder than I thought it would be. Sometimes I just want to fit in and make my life easy. Give me the courage to take up my cross today. Help me to see You as a treasure so beautiful that I'm willing to let go of whatever holds me back. Amen.

My Notes & Thoughts

Brick #32: Suffering: Where Is God When It Hurts?

Cold Open Moment

You are sitting on the edge of your bed, staring blankly at the wall. The house is entirely quiet now, but the echo of the shouting from downstairs is still ringing in your ears. The word "divorce" was finally said out loud, and suddenly, the floor dropped out from under your life.

Or maybe for you, it was the text message saying your friend's mom didn't make it. Or the doctor explaining why you won't be able to play your sport ever again. Or the suffocating wave of anxiety that pins you to your mattress for no logical reason.

When the pain hits, the Sunday School answers suddenly feel completely empty. If God is entirely good, and God is entirely powerful, why is this happening? Why didn't He stop it? When your life is shattering, the silence from heaven can feel absolutely deafening.

Big Idea

God does not always explain *why* we suffer, but He promises to be with us in the pain and guarantees that suffering will not have the final word.

Why This Matters

If your theology can't handle a hospital waiting room, a funeral home, or a panic attack, it isn't real theology. Understanding a biblical view of suffering matters because:

- It gives you permission to be sad, angry, and confused without feeling like a "bad Christian."
- It protects you from the toxic lie that your suffering is just karma for a mistake you made.
- It equips you to actually comfort your friends when they are hurting, instead of offering them cringey clichés.

Key Words

The Fall: The moment human beings rebelled against God, fracturing everything. It is the reason the world is infected with disease, cruelty, natural disasters, and death. *Precision Note: Rooted in Genesis 3, this refers to the introduction of systemic physical and spiritual corruption into the human experience.*

Lament: A passionate, unfiltered expression of grief, anger, or sorrow directed toward God. *Precision Note: A major biblical genre comprising roughly a third of the Psalms, demonstrating that God welcomes our raw emotional pain.*

The Incarnation: The historic event where the eternal Son of God became a human being in Jesus Christ. *Precision Note: The union of divine and human natures in the single person of Christ, meaning God has physically experienced human suffering.*

Bible Receipts

John 11:33–35 *"When Jesus saw her crying, and the Jews who had come with her crying, he was deeply angered in his spirit and deeply moved... Jesus wept."* This is the shortest verse in the Bible, and maybe the most profound. Jesus is minutes away from raising His friend Lazarus from the dead. He already knows the happy ending is coming. But when He sees the grief of Mary and Martha, He doesn't tell them to cheer up. He stands in the dirt and cries with them.

Revelation 21:4 *"He will wipe away every tear from their eyes. Death will be no more; grief, crying, and pain will be no more, because the previous things have passed away."* This is the finish line. The Bible does not promise that our current lives will be pain-free, but it absolutely guarantees that our eternity will be. God is keeping track of your tears, and one day, He will permanently eliminate the things that caused them.

Truth in Plain English

When Christians don't know what to say to someone who is hurting, they often say incredibly stupid things. Have you ever heard someone say, "Well, everything happens for a reason," or "God just needed another angel in heaven"?

Those phrases aren't in the Bible. In fact, they are lies.

God did not design the world to have cancer, bullying, car crashes, or depression. Those things exist because we live in a deeply broken, fallen world. **God does not ask you to fake a smile when your heart is breaking.** He isn't looking down from heaven expecting you to pretend everything is fine.

Instead, God offers us something much better than a quick explanation. He offers us Himself.

Look at other worldviews. In some religions, god is distant and untouchable. In secularism, suffering is just meaningless, random bad luck. But Christianity is radically different. **Jesus didn't just shout good advice from the safety of heaven; He came down and bled with us.** Jesus knows what it feels like to be betrayed by a best friend. He knows physical torture. He knows what it feels like to cry out to God and hear silence. When you are suffering, you are not praying to a boss who can't relate to you. You are praying to a Savior with scars on His hands.

Sometimes, God rescues us *from* the fire. He heals the sickness or fixes the family. But often, God chooses to walk *through* the fire with us. **God's ultimate answer to our suffering is not a detailed explanation, but His own presence.** We can hold onto hope because we know the end of the story: Jesus walked out of the grave, which means death and pain have an expiration date.

Common Confusion Box

What people think: If I am suffering, it means God is mad at me or He is punishing me for a sin I committed. **Why it sounds right:** It feels like karma. When we do something bad, we expect bad things to happen to us as payback. **Why it's wrong:** While our foolish choices can definitely cause painful consequences (like getting a failing grade because you didn't study), random suffering is not God "getting back at you." Jesus took all the punishment for your sins on the cross. God's anger toward you is gone. **What Scripture shows instead:** In John 9, Jesus's followers asked if a man was born blind because of his own sin or his parents' sin. Jesus explicitly said, "Neither." He broke the idea that suffering is always a direct punishment.

Why This Changes Real Life

Knowing how God handles suffering completely transforms how you handle your own pain.

First, it means you can learn how to lament. You can scream in your car, write angry journal entries to God, and cry until your chest hurts. Read Psalm 88, it ends with the writer essentially saying, "Darkness is my only friend left." God put that in the Bible on purpose. He can handle your anger and your questions.

Second, it changes how you treat your friends when they are hurting. You don't have to be the "fixer." When your friend's parents split up, or when they are battling intense anxiety, you don't need a perfectly formulated theological argument. You just need to show up.

Sit on the couch with them. Bring them food. Play video games in silence. Cry when they cry. You represent Jesus best to a hurting friend not by giving a lecture, but by giving them your presence.

Try This This Week

Write your own Psalm of Lament. Take out a piece of paper or open a blank note on your phone. Be brutally honest with God about something that is hurting you, frustrating you, or confusing you right now. Do not use polite "church" words. Tell Him exactly how you feel. Finish the note by writing: "I don't understand this, but I am choosing to trust that You are with me."

Talk It Out

- **Easy:** What is the most unhelpful or annoying thing people say when someone is going through a hard time?
- **Real:** How do you normally react when life gets hard? Do you get angry, do you isolate yourself, or do you pretend you're fine?
- **Hard:** Is there a specific painful event in your life that makes it difficult for you to trust that God is actually good?
- **Group-Friendly:** How can this specific group do a better job of supporting each other when one of us is hurting, instead of just trying to "fix" it?

BELIEF BUILDER

(Write these down in your notes, this is your brick for this chapter!)

- **My one-sentence belief:** "I believe we live in a broken world where suffering is real, but God suffers with me and will one day wipe away every tear."
- **Bible receipts:** John 11:35; Revelation 21:4.
- **This changes my life because:** I don't have to fake being okay; I can bring my raw, honest pain directly to God.
- **One question I still have:** If God knows how much pain a tragedy will cause, why does He allow it to happen in the first place?

Short Prayer

Father, this world is so heavy sometimes. There is so much pain that makes no sense to me. When my heart is breaking, please keep me from pulling away from You. Remind me that Jesus knows exactly what suffering feels like. Help me to trust You in the dark, and give me the strength to just be there for my friends when they are hurting. Amen.

My Notes & Thoughts

Brick #33: Wisdom: Decisions Without Fear

Cold Open Moment

You are staring at the ceiling at 2:00 AM, completely paralyzed by a decision. Maybe it's about where to go to college. Maybe it's about whether you should break up with the person you're dating. Or maybe it's just deciding which friend group to invest in this year.

You've prayed about it. You've asked God to give you a sign. You've randomly opened your Bible hoping a verse would literally point to the answer. But all you hear is silence.

And underneath the silence is a suffocating fear: *What if I choose the wrong thing? What if I step out of God's will and ruin the rest of my life?* You feel like you are walking a tightrope blindfolded, terrified that one wrong step will send you crashing to the ground.

Big Idea

God's will is not a tightrope you can accidentally fall off of; it is a wide-open field of freedom bordered by the protective fences of His Word.

Why This Matters

If you think God is playing a cosmic game of hide-and-seek with your future, you will live in constant anxiety. Understanding biblical wisdom matters because:

- It frees you from the paralyzing fear of making a "wrong" decision.
- It stops you from looking for weird, superstitious "signs" from God.
- It empowers you to make confident choices based on character rather than circumstance.

Key Words

Wisdom: The practical skill of living life well in God's world; knowing what is right, what is good, and how to apply it to real-life situations. *Precision Note: In Hebrew, the word is hokmah, which was often used to describe the skill of an expert craftsman or artist, applied to the art of living.*

Discernment: The ability to judge well between multiple options, especially when choosing between "good" and "best" rather than just "right" and "wrong." *Precision Note: A spiritual sensitivity cultivated by the Holy Spirit and deep familiarity with Scripture.*

Revealed Will: The clear commands and instructions God has already given us in the Bible (e.g., love your enemies, do not steal, flee sexual immorality). *Precision Note: Distinguished from God's "hidden will" or "sovereign will," which includes the secret details of the future that He does not owe us explanations for.*

Bible Receipts

Proverbs 3:5–6 *"Trust in the Lord with all your heart, and do not rely on your own understanding; in all your ways know him, and he will make your paths straight."* This doesn't mean God will hand you a GPS with turn-by-turn directions for your life. It means that when your heart is locked onto trusting God and obeying what He has already commanded, your life will move in the right general direction.

James 1:5 *"Now if any of you lacks wisdom, he should ask God, who gives to all generously and ungrudgingly, and it will be given to him."* God loves it when we ask for wisdom. Notice what James says: God gives it *generously* and *ungrudgingly*. He isn't annoyed by your confusion. He wants to help you navigate your life, but He usually does it by giving you wisdom to choose, not a magic voice from the sky telling you what to do.

Truth in Plain English

A lot of us treat God like a Magic 8-Ball. We shake Him up, ask a specific question ("Should I date them?"), and wait for a mystical answer to float to the top. When it doesn't happen, we panic.

But God rarely gives us a flaming bush or a voice from heaven. Why? Because He is raising adults, not programming robots. **God cares much more about *who* you are becoming than *where* you are going.** Think of God's revealed will in the Bible like the strong fences of a massive pasture. The Bible clearly tells us things we must do (tell the truth, love others, serve the poor) and things we must avoid (gossip, lust, cruelty). Those are the fences.

But what about the space inside the fences? That is your freedom. **As long as you are staying within the boundaries of God's Word, you are free to choose what you want to do.** Should you be an engineer or a graphic designer? Should you go to the state school or get a job right away? If both options are within the fences of God's revealed will, He looks at you and says, "Which one do you want? Use the brain I gave you, ask wise people for advice, and go for it!"

You don't have to live in fear of missing God's will when you are actively obeying the commands He has already given you. If you are pursuing holiness, serving your church, and loving your neighbor, you can make a decision and sleep perfectly well at night. God's grace is big enough to catch you even if your choice doesn't pan out the way you hoped.

Common Confusion Box

What people think: I have a "soulmate" or one perfect path for my life, and if I miss it, I will have to settle for God's "Plan B." **Why it sounds right:** It sounds romantic and spiritual to think God has one specific college, one specific job, and one specific spouse secretly picked out for you to guess. **Why it's wrong:** The Bible never teaches this! If God wants you somewhere specific, He is entirely capable of getting you there. You cannot accidentally derail God's sovereign plan for the universe by picking the wrong major. **What Scripture shows instead:** Psalm 37:4 says, "Take delight in the Lord, and he will give you your heart's desires." When your heart is submitted to God, He actually trusts you to make choices based on your holy desires.

Why This Changes Real Life

When you stop looking for a magical sign, you can start using actual wisdom.

Let's say you have two good options in front of you. Instead of paralyzing yourself with anxiety, you can run those options through a "Wisdom Filter." You ask yourself: Does the Bible specifically command or forbid this? (If no, keep going). Which option better helps me love God and love people? What do my parents, my youth pastor, or my godly friends think I should do? What am I genuinely excited about?

Once you answer those questions, you just make the choice. You take a deep breath, make a move, and trust that God is walking with you.

This takes an incredible amount of pressure off your shoulders. It means your identity isn't riding on whether or not you get into a specific program or secure a specific date. You are already loved, already secure, and already in God's will simply by trusting Jesus. The rest is just an adventure you get to figure out with the Holy Spirit's help.

Try This This Week

Take one decision you are stressing out about right now. Stop asking God for a "sign" about it. Instead, take two mature, older Christians (a parent, a leader, a mentor) out for coffee or text them. Ask them: "I have a decision to make. Based on what you know about my character, my strengths, and my weaknesses, what do you think would be the wisest choice?" Listen to their answers without arguing.

Talk It Out

- **Easy:** Have you ever tried to "fleece" God by asking for a highly specific, weird sign to help you make a decision? What happened?
- **Real:** What is the biggest decision weighing on your mind right now? Why does it feel so heavy?
- **Hard:** Is it possible that you are using "I'm waiting on God's timing" as an excuse to avoid making a hard choice or having a hard conversation?
- **Group-Friendly:** How can we help each other make wise choices without acting like we know God's secret will for each other's lives?

BELIEF BUILDER

(Write these down in your notes, this is your brick for this chapter!)

- **My one-sentence belief:** "I believe God gives me the freedom to make wise choices within the boundaries of His Word, without fear of missing His plan."
- **Bible receipts:** Proverbs 3:5-6; James 1:5.
- **This changes my life because:** I don't have to live with decision-paralysis; I can ask for wisdom, make a choice, and trust God's grace.
- **One question I still have:** What do I do when I ask for wisdom from two different mature Christians and they give me total opposite advice?

Short Prayer

God, thank You for not making my life a guessing game. Forgive me for treating You like a Magic 8-Ball when You really want me to grow in wisdom. When I am facing a hard choice this week, calm my anxiety. Help me to stay inside the fences of Your Word, and give me the courage to make decisions with confidence. Amen.

My Notes & Thoughts

PART 8 - CHECKPOINT

Assemble Your Statement: "About the Christian Life"

You've made it through Part 8! Over the last three chapters, you've gathered some massive "bricks" regarding what it actually looks like to follow Jesus in the real world, how to handle the cost, how to process suffering, and how to make wise decisions without having a panic attack.

Now, it's time to take those individual bricks and cement them together into the 9th section of your Personal Statement of Faith.

Step 1: Review Your Bricks

Look back at the **BELIEF BUILDER** notes you wrote down at the end of Chapters 1, 2, and 3.

- **Chapter 1 (The Cost):** What did you write about giving up your right to run your own life and trusting Jesus as your ultimate treasure?
- **Chapter 2 (Suffering):** What did you write about God suffering with us and the promise that He will one day wipe away every tear?
- **Chapter 3 (Wisdom):** What did you write about the freedom to make wise choices within the boundaries of His Word without fear?

Step 2: The Cleanup Phase

Before you combine these sentences, let's tighten them up.

- **Circle the duplicates:** Did you use the word "trust" four different times? Swap one out for "rely on" or "have confidence in."
- **Replace the "stuff":** If you used words like "bad stuff" or "hard times," upgrade your vocabulary. Use theological words you've learned, like *suffering*, *lament*, *cost*, or *discernment*.

Step 3: Combine and Polish

Now, weave your three bricks together into one solid paragraph under the heading **About the Christian Life**. Add transition words (like *because*, *however*, or *therefore*) so it reads smoothly.

Example Draft: *"I believe following Jesus means giving up my right to run my own life, but He is a treasure worth any cost. We live in a broken world where suffering is real, but I can lament honestly because God suffers with me and will one day wipe away every tear. Because I am secure in Him, God gives me the freedom to make wise choices within the boundaries of His Word, without the paralyzing fear of missing His plan."*

Step 4: The 15-Second Spoken Rep

The goal isn't just to write this down; it's to be able to actually say it out loud when life gets hard or when a friend asks you how you handle stress.

Take your paragraph and shrink it down to two sentences you can say in 15 seconds.

Example Spoken Script: *"Following Jesus costs me my comfort, but He's worth it. Even when life gets painfully hard or confusing, I don't have to panic, because God promises to walk through the suffering with me and gives me the wisdom I need to make the next right choice."*

Practice it right now: Stand up, look in the mirror, and say your short version out loud twice. Don't skip this! Speaking your theology out loud makes it real.

My Statement of Faith (after part 8)

PART 9 - LAST THINGS: Hope That Doesn't Break

In this part, we're looking at the future, not as a scary topic, but as fuel for courage. We'll talk about death, resurrection, judgment, and the promise of new creation, so your hope isn't just "I go to heaven someday," but "God will make all things right." The goal is to help you write an "About the Future" section that gives you steadiness when life feels unfair and confidence that evil doesn't get the final word. This part is about hope that actually holds.

Brick #34: Death and What Happens Next

Cold Open Moment

You're scrolling through your feed, laughing at a meme, when suddenly you see a tribute post. Someone young died. Maybe it's a celebrity you followed, a kid from a rival high school, or a family member.

Suddenly, your thumb stops scrolling. The room feels a little too quiet, and a cold, heavy thought hits you: *I am going to die someday. Everyone I love is going to die someday.* It is a terrifying, suffocating thought. Most of the time, we try to drown that thought out with noise, music, sports, and constant busyness. But when the noise stops, the question is still sitting there waiting for you: What actually happens the second your heart stops beating?

Big Idea

Death is a tragic enemy that was never part of God's original design, but because Jesus defeated it, death is now just a doorway into His immediate presence.

Why This Matters

If you are secretly terrified of dying, or if you think heaven is just playing a harp on a boring cloud forever, it will drain the joy out of your life right now. Knowing the truth about death matters because:

- It removes the paralyzing fear of the unknown.
- It totally changes how you grieve when you lose someone you love.
- It gives you an incredible sense of urgency to make your life count today.

Key Words

Mortality: The state of being subject to death; the reality that our physical bodies will eventually fail and die. *Precision Note: Physical death was introduced to the human race as a direct consequence of the Fall (Genesis 3), severing the body from the soul.*

The Intermediate State: The temporary period of time between a person's physical death and the future day when Jesus returns to resurrect our bodies. *Precision Note: During this time, the souls of believers are fully conscious and in the immediate presence of Christ, awaiting their new physical bodies.*

Bible Receipts

Philippians 1:21–23 *"For me, to live is Christ and to die is gain... I have the desire to depart and be with Christ, which is very much better."* The Apostle Paul was sitting in a Roman prison when he wrote this, facing possible execution. He wasn't suicidal, but he also wasn't afraid. He realized that living meant he got to serve Jesus, but dying meant he got to actually *be* with Jesus. To Paul, dying wasn't a tragedy; it was an upgrade.

2 Corinthians 5:8 *"We are confident, I say, and would prefer to be away from the body and at home with the Lord."* This destroys the idea of "soul sleep" (the false idea that when you die, you just go unconscious until the end of the world). Paul makes it clear: the very second your soul leaves your physical body, it is immediately at home with Jesus. There is no waiting room.

Truth in Plain English

We need to be painfully honest about something: death is awful. It is ugly, sad, and entirely unnatural.

God created humans to have a physical body and a soul perfectly knit together forever. **Death is an invader that rips apart what God meant to stay together.** This is why funerals feel so incredibly wrong. You were not wired to say goodbye to the people you love.

But here is the massive plot twist of Christianity: **Jesus hijacked death.**

When Jesus died on the cross and walked out of the tomb three days later, He broke the back of death. **For a Christian, death is no longer a brick wall at the end of your life; Jesus turned it into a doorway.** What happens when you walk through that doorway? Your physical body is buried, but your soul, the core of who you actually are, goes instantly to be with Jesus. You don't lose your personality. You don't turn into a ghost. You are fully awake, completely yourself, and experiencing a joy and peace that is impossible to describe. **You are more alive the second after you die than you ever were on earth.**

Common Confusion Box

What people think: When good people die, they turn into angels and get their wings. **Why it sounds right:** We see it in movies, cartoons, and on greeting cards all the time. People often say things like, "Heaven gained another angel today." **Why it's wrong:** Humans and angels are two entirely different types of beings. When a dog dies, it doesn't turn into a human. When a human dies, they don't turn into an angel. **What Scripture shows instead:** God made you human on purpose! Humans are the crown of His creation, not "pre-angels." When you die, your soul goes to heaven, but you remain human. In fact, 1 Corinthians 6:3 mind-blowingly hints that one day, humans will actually *judge* the angels.

Why This Changes Real Life

Knowing what happens after death completely changes how you stand beside a casket at a funeral.

When a Christian you love dies, it is okay to cry. It is okay to be furious that they are gone. Remember, Jesus wept at His friend's tomb even though He knew the ending! Grief is the price we pay for love.

But as a Christian, your grief has a safety net. 1 Thessalonians 4:13 says that we grieve, but not "like those who have no hope." You know that the person you love is currently more alive, more safe, and more joyful than they have ever been.

It also changes how you live your random Tuesday afternoons. If this life is just the opening credits to an eternal movie, you don't have to desperately try to cram every single experience into your teenage years. You don't have to be paralyzed by FOMO (Fear Of Missing Out) or the crushing pressure to "peak" in high school, because you know the absolute best part of your life hasn't even started yet.

Try This This Week

Have a completely honest 5-minute conversation with a Christian parent, youth leader, or mentor. Give them a quick heads-up first ("Hey, I'm reading a book about some heavy stuff..."), and then ask them this exact question: "When you think about the future, are you afraid of dying? Why or why not?" Listen to how someone older than you processes their own mortality through the lens of their faith.

Talk It Out

- **Easy:** What is the most ridiculous or funny thing you used to believe about heaven when you were a little kid?
- **Real:** When you think about dying someday, what is the biggest fear or anxiety that pops into your head?
- **Hard:** If you truly believed that "to die is gain" (like Paul said), how would it change the way you stress out about your future right now?
- **Group-Friendly:** Based on what we just read, what is one Christian cliché we need to *stop* saying when someone is grieving, and what is one practical thing we should *start* doing instead?

BELIEF BUILDER

(Write these down in your notes, this is your first brick for the "About the Future" section!)

- **My one-sentence belief:** "I believe that physical death is a defeated enemy, and when a Christian dies, their soul goes immediately to be with Jesus."
- **Bible receipts:** Philippians 1:21; 2 Corinthians 5:8.
- **This changes my life because:** I don't have to be paralyzed by the fear of death, and I can grieve with absolute hope.
- **One question I still have:** If my soul is in heaven with Jesus, what happens to my physical body forever?

Short Prayer

Lord, the idea of death honestly scares me sometimes. I hate losing people I love, and I don't fully understand how it all works. But I thank You that Jesus defeated the grave. Thank You that death does not get the final word. When I feel anxious about the future, remind me that my soul is safe with You. Amen.

My Notes & Thoughts

Brick #35: Resurrection and Judgment

Cold Open Moment

You are watching the news or reading an article, and your blood starts to boil. A corrupt billionaire got away with stealing life savings from ordinary people. A notorious abuser avoided jail time on a technicality. The school bully graduated with honors and no one ever found out how much they destroyed the mental health of other students.

You feel a burning sense of outrage in your chest. It feels like the universe is broken. It feels like the bad guys actually win.

When you see raw injustice, your instinct is to want revenge. You want someone to level the playing field. Does God care about the people who get crushed by history? Does evil just get swept under the rug forever?

Big Idea

Jesus is returning to resurrect our physical bodies, right every wrong, and judge the world with perfect justice and mercy.

Why This Matters

People get extremely uncomfortable when you mention the word "judgment." It sounds aggressive. But understanding final judgment matters because it frees you from the exhausting burden of trying to take revenge yourself. It guarantees that the villains of history do not get the final word. Furthermore, the promise of resurrection proves that your physical body matters deeply to God, which radically changes how you view yourself in the mirror.

Key Words

Resurrection: The future event where God will raise the physical bodies of all people from the dead, reuniting them with their souls. *Precision Note: At Christ's return, believers will receive glorified, immortal bodies patterned after Jesus's own resurrected body (1 Corinthians 15).*

Final Judgment: The moment at the end of history when Jesus will perfectly and fairly evaluate every human life. *Precision Note: A cosmic event that publically vindicates God's righteousness and permanently eliminates evil from the universe.*

Hell: Eternal separation from the presence, goodness, and grace of God. *Precision Note: A state of active judgment against unrepentant rebellion, where those who rejected God are given exactly what they demanded: existence without Him.*

Bible Receipts

1 Corinthians 15:52–53 *"For the trumpet will sound, the dead will be raised imperishable, and we will be changed. For this corruptible body must be clothed with incorruptibility, and this mortal body must be clothed with immortality."* When Jesus returns, your soul isn't going to just float around forever. God is going to raise your physical body from the grave and give it a massive upgrade. It will be "imperishable", meaning it will never get sick, break down, get tired, or die again.

Revelation 20:11–12 *"Then I saw a great white throne and one seated on it... I also saw the dead, the great and the small, standing before the throne, and books were opened."* This is the ultimate courtroom scene. Every human being who has ever lived will stand before Jesus. Nothing will be hidden. Every secret text, every hidden abuse, and every act of kindness will be brought into the light. Justice will finally be served perfectly.

Truth in Plain English

If God never judged evil, He wouldn't be a good God. Think about it. **A God who doesn't get angry at abuse, cruelty, and racism is a God who doesn't actually love people.** When Jesus returns, He is going to permanently expel evil, sin, and death from reality. For people who have spent their entire lives running from God and rejecting His grace, they will be given exactly what they asked for: an eternity completely separated from Him. That is what Hell is.

But for a Christian, the Final Judgment isn't something to be terrified of. Why? Because Jesus already stood trial for you. **Because Jesus took your punishment on the cross, Judgment Day isn't your condemnation; it is your vindication.** You will stand before the throne clothed in the perfect record of Jesus.

Not only that, but God is going to give you your body back. **Your physical body isn't a temporary rental car; it is the permanent home God designed for your soul.** God is going to resurrect you, heal every physical flaw, erase every disease, and make your body completely indestructible.

Common Confusion Box

What people think: Hell is an underground torture chamber where the devil rules with a pitchfork. **Why it sounds right:** This is how Hell is drawn in hundreds of cartoons, comic books, and old medieval paintings. **Why it's wrong:** Satan isn't the king of Hell; he is a prisoner there. God didn't originally create Hell for humans, but for the devil and his demons. **What Scripture shows instead:** 2 Thessalonians 1:9 describes Hell as paying the penalty of eternal destruction "from the Lord's presence and from his glorious strength." Hell is the tragic reality of God honoring a person's lifelong demand to be left completely alone.

Why This Changes Real Life

This doctrine has two massive, practical impacts on your life right now.

First, you can stop obsessing over your body image. We spend so much time stressing in front of the mirror, hating our acne, our weight, or our physical limitations. When you realize that this current body is just a rough draft of the glorious, immortal body you will receive at the resurrection, it takes the pressure off.

Second, you can actually let go of grudges. When someone deeply wrongs you, you don't have to spend your energy trying to ruin their life in return. Romans 12 says, "Vengeance belongs to me; I will repay, says the Lord." You can hand your anger over to Jesus, trusting that He will handle justice far better than you ever could.

Try This This Week

Is there someone you are holding a quiet grudge against? Maybe a friend who ghosted you or someone who lied about you? Write their name down on a piece of paper. Pray specifically that God would show them mercy, and intentionally surrender your right to get revenge. Then, physically cross their name out as a sign that you are letting Jesus handle the justice.

Talk It Out

1. **Easy:** If you could pick one physical upgrade for your resurrected body (like never needing sleep, running without getting tired, etc.), what would it be?
2. **Real:** Why does the idea of "Judgment Day" usually make Christians feel terrified instead of relieved?
3. **Hard:** Do you struggle with wanting revenge when someone hurts you? How does knowing Jesus will judge the world change how you react to being wronged?
4. **Group-Friendly:** How can we remind each other of the resurrection when we are dealing with physical sickness, injuries, or body-image insecurities?

BELIEF BUILDER

(Write these down in your notes, this is your second brick for the "About the Future" section!)

- **My one-sentence belief:** "I believe Jesus will return to resurrect our physical bodies, judge evil perfectly, and wipe out injustice forever."
- **Bible receipts:** 1 Corinthians 15:52-53; Revelation 20:11-12.
- **This changes my life because:** I can let go of my need for revenge, and I can stop hating my physical flaws.
- **One question I still have:** What will we actually be doing with our resurrected bodies forever?

Short Prayer

Jesus, the world is full of so much unfairness and pain. Thank You for promising that evil will not win. Thank You that You took the judgment I deserved on the cross. Help me to let go of the grudges I'm holding onto, and give me hope knowing that one day You will make all things right and make my body new. Amen.

My Notes & Thoughts

Brick #36: New Creation

Cold Open Moment

Be entirely honest: when you picture Heaven, do you picture a really long, extremely boring church service?

Do you picture sitting on a fluffy white cloud, wearing a white robe, and strumming a golden harp for ten trillion years? If that is what you think eternity looks like, it makes total sense that you aren't that excited to go there. In fact, you might even be a little bummed out, thinking, *Man, I really hope Jesus waits to come back until after I get my driver's license, fall in love, and go to college.*

We have totally bought into the lie that the physical world is fun and exciting, while the spiritual world is boring and weird. But what if the ultimate goal of history isn't for us to leave earth forever? What if the goal is for Heaven to come down here?

Big Idea

Heaven isn't a boring cloud you float on forever; it is a physical, resurrected Earth where we will live, work, and rule with God.

Why This Matters

Knowing the true endgame of history gives you a massive sense of hope when the world feels irreparably dark. It gives incredible meaning to your hobbies, your art, your sports, and your future career because you realize God deeply values the physical world. Instead of thinking, "I can't wait to escape this place," biblical hope shifts your mindset to, "I can't wait for Jesus to fix this place."

Key Words

New Heavens and New Earth: The final, eternal state of the universe where God's realm and the human realm are permanently fused together in physical perfection. *Precision Note: Described in Revelation 21, this represents the culmination of God's redemptive plan to dwell directly with humanity.*

Restoration: The process of taking something broken and returning it to its original, perfect design. *Precision Note: The Greek word palingenesia, meaning "rebirth" or "renewal" of the cosmos, showing God redeems creation rather than scrapping it.*

Shalom: The Hebrew concept of universal flourishing, wholeness, and absolute peace where nothing is missing and nothing is broken. *Precision Note: It goes far beyond the absence of conflict; it is the vibrant, joyous harmony of humans, nature, and God.*

Bible Receipts

Revelation 21:1–3 *"Then I saw a new heaven and a new earth; for the first heaven and the first earth had passed away... I heard a loud voice from the throne: 'Look, God's dwelling is with humanity, and he will live with them.'"* Notice the direction here. We do not fly away to live in God's spiritual realm. God brings His realm *down* to the new earth to live with us. Heaven is God coming to live in our neighborhood permanently.

Romans 8:21 *"That the creation itself will also be set free from the bondage to decay into the glorious freedom of God's children."* The physical planet, the oceans, mountains, forests, and animals, are currently suffering under the curse of sin. But Paul says the earth itself is going to be set free. God loves the planet He made, and He is going to rescue it, not destroy it.

Truth in Plain English

God is not going to throw the earth in the cosmic trash can. **God isn't scrapping the universe; He is scrubbing it clean of sin, death, and decay.** The eternal state of a Christian isn't a ghost floating in the sky. It is a resurrected human, living on a resurrected earth, in the presence of a resurrected Jesus. The New Earth will be profoundly physical. We will eat incredible food, build beautiful things, create art, explore mountains, and laugh with our friends.

There will be a massive, glowing city called the New Jerusalem. There will be culture, music, and architecture, but without any pollution, crime, greed, or injustice. You will finally get to be exactly who God created you to be, without the constant weight of anxiety or temptation holding you down.

Heaven is not the end of the adventure; it is simply chapter one of the real story God has been writing since the beginning. Everything good you experience right now, a perfect sunset, a massive laugh with your best friend, a brilliant piece of music, is just an appetizer for the New Earth.

Common Confusion Box

What people think: The physical world doesn't matter because it's all going to burn up eventually anyway. **Why it sounds right:** Christians often focus entirely on "saving souls" and forget that God also cares about physical bodies and the environment. **Why it's wrong:** Believing the physical world is "bad" and the spiritual world is "good" is an ancient heresy called Gnosticism. God called the physical world "very good" in Genesis 1! **What Scripture shows instead:** Colossians 1:20 says that Jesus shed His blood on the cross to reconcile *all things* to Himself, "whether things on earth or things in heaven."

Why This Changes Real Life

If you know the world is going to be resurrected, it changes how you treat the world right now.

It means your work actually matters. When you paint a picture, write a song, engineer a bridge, or clean up a park, you are practicing for eternity. You are bringing a tiny sliver of *Shalom* into a broken world. God cares about culture and beauty.

It also gives you an anchor on your darkest days. When you get a devastating medical diagnosis, or when your heart is broken, you can look forward and know that the story doesn't end in the dark. The sun is going to rise on a New Earth. Every tear will be wiped away. Everything sad is going to come untrue.

Try This This Week

Go outside for ten minutes without your phone. Find one beautiful thing in nature, a massive tree, a complex leaf, the stars, or a sunset. Take a deep breath and tell God, "If this is what Your broken world looks like, I can't wait to see the restored one."

Talk It Out

1. **Easy:** If there are animals on the New Earth, what is the first animal you want to safely hang out with?
2. **Real:** How does the idea of a physical, active New Earth change how you feel about eternity? Does it make you more excited?
3. **Hard:** If God values the physical world so much that He plans to restore it, how should that change how we treat the environment and our communities right now?
4. **Group-Friendly:** What is one "appetizer" in your life right now (a favorite meal, hobby, or experience) that makes you excited for the full banquet of the New Creation?

BELIEF BUILDER

(Write these down in your notes, this is your final brick for the "About the Future" section!)

- **My one-sentence belief:** "I believe God will permanently unite heaven and earth, restoring the physical world so we can live with Him forever in perfect joy."
- **Bible receipts:** Revelation 21:1-3; Romans 8:21.
- **This changes my life because:** It gives meaning to the physical work and art I do now, and proves the story ends with a beautiful beginning.
- **One question I still have:** Will we remember our old, painful lives when we are on the New Earth?

Short Prayer

Father, thank You that the story doesn't end in a graveyard. Thank You that You love this world enough to restore it. Whenever I feel hopeless or overwhelmed by the news, remind me of the New Heavens and the New Earth. Help me to bring tiny pieces of Your kingdom into my school and my home today. Amen.

My Notes & Thoughts

PART 9 - CHECKPOINT

Assemble Your Statement: "About the Future"

You made it to the end of the theological heavy lifting! Over the last three chapters, you explored the endgame of Christianity. You dismantled the myths about death, faced the reality of Judgment Day, and caught a glimpse of the resurrected New Earth.

Now, it's time to take those three final bricks and cement them together into the 10th and final section of your Personal Statement of Faith.

Step 1: Review Your Bricks

Look back at the **BELIEF BUILDER** notes you wrote down at the end of Chapters 1, 2, and 3.

- **Chapter 1 (Death):** What did you write about death being defeated and the soul going to be with Jesus?
- **Chapter 2 (Resurrection/Judgment):** What did you write about Jesus returning to resurrect our bodies and judge evil perfectly?
- **Chapter 3 (New Creation):** What did you write about God uniting heaven and earth to restore the physical world forever?

Step 2: The Cleanup Phase

Before you combine these sentences, let's tighten the bolts.

- **Circle the duplicates:** Did you use the word "forever" or "physical" too many times? Smooth it out.
- **Replace the "stuff":** If you used words like "bad guys" or "boring clouds," upgrade your vocabulary. Use the sharp theological words you've learned: *mortality, intermediate state, resurrection, final judgment, restoration,* or *shalom*.

Step 3: Combine and Polish

Weave your three bricks together into one solid, powerful paragraph under the heading **About the Future**. Add transition words to make it read like a triumphant finale.

Example Draft: *"I believe that physical death is a defeated enemy, and when a Christian dies, their soul goes immediately to be with Jesus. Ultimately, Jesus will return to resurrect our physical bodies, judge evil perfectly, and wipe out injustice forever. He will permanently unite heaven and earth, restoring the physical world so we can live with Him in perfect shalom and joy."*

Step 4: The 15-Second Spoken Rep

This is your final 15-second rep before the Capstone. Condense this massive theological hope into two sentences you can say to a friend who asks you what you believe about the end of the world.

Example Spoken Script: *"I believe death isn't the end. Jesus is returning to resurrect our bodies, destroy all evil, and restore the earth so we can live with Him in a perfect physical world forever."*

Practice it right now: Stand up, look in the mirror, and say your short version out loud twice. Let the reality of that hope actually sink into your chest!

My Statement of Faith (after part 9)

PART 10 - CAPSTONE: ASSEMBLE YOUR STATEMENT OF FAITH

This is where everything you've been building finally becomes something you can hold. In this part, you're going to take every "brick" you wrote along the way and **assemble it into your Personal Statement of Faith**, clear, organized, and in your own words. We'll walk step-by-step through how to tighten your sentences, remove repeats, add the right Bible "receipts," and shape your beliefs into a **1-page statement** you can actually be proud of. Then we'll help you compress it into a **30-second version** you can speak naturally, and we'll build your **"When I Doubt" plan** so you're not guessing what to do when faith feels shaky. The goal isn't to make you sound like a theologian, it's to help you live like someone who knows what they believe, why they believe it, and how to return to truth when life gets loud.

Brick #37: Build Your 1-Page Statement

Cold Open Moment

Take a deep breath and look back at what you have just done. Over the past several weeks, you haven't just passively read a book. You've wrestled with ancient truths, asked hard questions, and literally built your own theology from the ground up.

Most adults go their entire lives without doing what you just did.

But right now, your theology is probably scattered across ten different checkpoints, saved in the notes app on your phone, or scribbled in the margins of a notebook. It's time to bring all those pieces together. It is time to assemble your house.

Big Idea

Your Personal Statement of Faith is a stake in the ground, a permanent reminder of what is true when your emotions, your circumstances, or the world try to tell you otherwise.

Step-by-Step Assembly

Step 1: Gather the 10 Bricks Open up your notes and locate the final paragraphs you wrote at the end of every Part. You should have exactly ten paragraphs.

Step 2: Plug Them Into the Framework Create a new, blank document. Give it a title:

"Your Name"

's Personal Statement of Faith. Underneath the title, you are going to paste your ten paragraphs under these specific headings. Do not skip any!

1. **About the Bible:** (Paste Checkpoint 1 here)
2. **About God:** (Paste Checkpoint 2 here)
3. **About Jesus:** (Paste Checkpoint 4 here)
4. **About the Holy Spirit:** (Paste Checkpoint 6 here)
5. **About People:** (Paste the first half of Checkpoint 3 here)
6. **About Sin:** (Paste the second half of Checkpoint 3 here)
7. **About Salvation:** (Paste Checkpoint 5 here)
8. **About the Church:** (Paste Checkpoint 7 here)

9. **About the Christian Life:** (Paste Checkpoint 8 here)

10. **About the Future:** (Paste Checkpoint 9 here)

(Pro-tip: Include the Bible receipts you saved for each section right below your paragraphs! This anchors your statement firmly in Scripture.)

Step 3: The Final Polish Read the entire document from top to bottom out loud. Hearing your own voice say these words will help you realize this is your actual belief staring back at you.

- Does it sound like *you* wrote it? If any sentence sounds too much like a theology professor and not enough like you, change the wording so it fits your voice (just keep the truth the same).

- Are there any awkward transitions? Add words like *therefore*, *however*, or *because* to make it flow like one giant, unified story.

Step 4: Lock It In Print it out. Seriously, use real paper. Sign your name and today's date at the bottom. Put it inside your Bible, pin it to your bulletin board, or tape it inside your locker. You now have a 1-page anchor for your faith.

The 30-Second Faith

Why This Matters

Your 1-Page Statement is incredible for your own personal growth, but you probably aren't going to pull a piece of paper out of your pocket when you are eating lunch in the cafeteria.

When a friend asks you, "So, what do you actually believe?", or when someone challenges your faith online, you need to be able to explain the core of Christianity clearly, confidently, and quickly. You need a 30-Second Faith script.

Step-by-Step Assembly

Step 1: The Core Four You cannot summarize every single doctrine in 30 seconds. Instead, you need to focus on the four massive pillars of the Christian story:

- **God:** Who made us?

- **Sin:** What went wrong?

- **Jesus:** What did God do about it?

- **Hope:** How does the story end?

Step 2: Draft Your Script Look at your 1-Page Statement and pull out the absolute best, most crucial sentences that answer those four questions. Smash them together into a 3–4 sentence paragraph. (Don't just copy the example below, use the actual words you wrote so it sounds like you!)

Example 30-Second Script: *"I believe that a perfectly good God created the world, but human beings fractured it by choosing our own way, which brought sin and death into reality. But God didn't abandon us; Jesus, who is fully God and fully man, came down, took the punishment for our sin on the cross, and physically rose from the dead. Because of Jesus, I am forgiven entirely by grace, and I have the hope that one day He will return to restore the world and make everything new."*

Step 3: Practice It Out Loud Start a timer on your phone. Read your draft out loud at a normal, conversational speed. Did you stay under 30 seconds? Did it sound natural? Keep editing until it flows perfectly off your tongue.

Brick #38: The "When I Doubt" Plan

Big Idea

Doubt is not a sin; it is a normal part of growing up. But surviving doubt requires a practical game plan before the questions actually hit.

Why This Matters

Someday, maybe tomorrow, maybe in three years during a college class, or maybe after a massive tragedy strikes your family, you are going to wake up and feel completely numb. You will look at your Bible and think, *What if I made all of this up? What if none of this is actually true?*

When that happens, Satan wants you to panic, isolate yourself, and quit. God wants you to bring your questions directly to Him. If you build a "When I Doubt" Plan right now, while your faith is strong, you will know exactly what to do when the storm hits.

Build Your Plan

Fill out these four steps. Take out your phone and physically put this plan in your notes app so you never lose it.

1. The "Who" (Name Your People) Doubt grows in the dark. The second you speak a doubt out loud, it loses half of its power over you.

- *Write down the names of TWO mature Christians you completely trust.* (This could be a parent, a youth pastor, or an older mentor. Pick someone who knows how to listen and won't just throw cheap Christian clichés at you.)
- *Commitment:* "When I doubt, I will not hide it. I will text “Name 1” or “Name 2”

and say, 'I am struggling with my faith right now and I need to talk.'"

2. The "What" (Name Your Anchor) When you doubt the complex stuff (like how the Trinity works or why God allows suffering), you need to drop an anchor back to the simplest, most undeniable truth.

- *Write down your core anchor:* "When I am confused about the details, I will look at the resurrection. Jesus actually walked out of a real grave in history. If He beat death, I can trust Him with the rest."

3. The "Where" (Name Your Inputs) When you are doubting, scrolling through anti-Christian TikTok videos or arguing in comment sections will only make your anxiety worse. You need better inputs.

- *Write down ONE solid resource you will turn to:* (Ask your youth pastor or mentor for a recommendation, like a specific podcast, a YouTube channel, or a website like GotQuestions.org that does not read like a seminary textbook).

4. The "How" (Name Your Prayer) You don't need fancy faith to pray. You can pray with your doubts.

FINAL CHECKPOINT: Read It, Speak It, Live It

- *Commitment:* "When I doubt, I will pray exactly what the desperate father prayed in Mark 9:24: *'Lord, I believe; help my unbelief!'"*

This is it. You have constructed a massive, beautiful, storm-proof theology.

- **Read your 1-Page Statement** whenever you feel confused about who God is or who you are. Let it remind you of the truth.
- **Speak your 30-Second Script** whenever you get the chance to share the greatest story ever told. Do it with humility, warmth, and unshakeable confidence.
- **Live out your "When I Doubt" Plan** because following Jesus is the hardest, most beautiful adventure you will ever go on, and you cannot do it alone.

You know what you believe. Now, go live like it's true.

My Statement of Faith

Appendix: Your Personal Tools to Write

The appendix is where everything comes together. You'll get templates and examples to help you assemble your **30-Second Faith**, your **1-Page Personal Statement of Faith**, and your **Anchored (2–4 page) version** with Bible receipts. You'll also build your **"When I Doubt" plan** – a simple strategy you can use when you're spiraling or questioning. The goal is that you don't just finish this book feeling inspired, but that you finish with something concrete you can revisit, refine, and actually use for years.

Appendix A: Personal Statement Templates

Permission is granted to photocopy these templates for personal or small group use.

1. The 30-Second Faith Script Template

My Core Four Beliefs I believe that a perfectly good God created the world, but human beings fractured it by ____, which brought sin and death into reality.

But God didn't abandon us; Jesus, who is fully God and fully man, came down, ____ on the cross, and physically rose from the dead.

Because of Jesus, I am forgiven entirely by grace, and I have the hope that one day He will return to ____.

2. The 1-Page Statement Template

"Your Name's" Personal Statement of Faith *Date:* ______________

- **About the Bible:** I believe...
- **About God:** I believe...
- **About Jesus:** I believe...
- **About the Holy Spirit:** I believe...
- **About People:** I believe...
- **About Sin:** I believe...
- **About Salvation:** I believe...
- **About the Church:** I believe...
- **About the Christian Life:** I believe...
- **About the Future:** I believe...

3. The 2–4 Page Anchored Statement Template

(Use this expanded format if you want to include Scripture references and a short explanation of what your beliefs look like in real life).

Section 1: About God

- **My Belief:** I believe God is...
- **My Anchor (Bible Receipt):** ____________________ (e.g., Psalm 145:3)
- **What this means for my life:** Because God is like this, I don't have to... instead I can...

(Repeat this structure for all 10 headings).

4. The "When I Doubt" Plan Worksheet

My Game Plan for the Dark Days

Appendix B: Sample Statements of Faith

- **The "Who":** When I doubt my faith, I refuse to hide in the dark. I will text or call __ **and** __. I will tell them, "I am struggling and need to talk."
- **The "What":** When the complex theology confuses me, my core anchor is the undeniable truth that ______________________________.
- **The "Where":** When I am anxious about my beliefs, I will stop scrolling through comment sections and instead listen to/read ______________________________.
- **The "How":** When my faith feels weak, my honest prayer to God will be: "______________________________"

Here is how three different teenagers might write their 30-Second Faith scripts, depending on what their church background emphasizes. Notice that they all agree on the core truth, even though their wording leans a little differently!

Version 1: Broadly Evangelical / Credal "I believe in one God, Father, Son, and Holy Spirit, who created everything good. We ruined the world through our sin, but Jesus Christ, who is fully God and man, died for our sins and physically rose from the dead. I am saved by grace through faith in Him alone, and I am waiting for the day He returns to judge the world and make all things new."

Version 2: Reformed-Leaning (Gentle) "I believe God is completely sovereign and perfectly holy. Even when we were spiritually dead and running away from Him, God chose to rescue us anyway. Jesus lived the perfect life I couldn't, died on the cross to take the punishment my sin deserved, and rose from the grave to conquer death. I am saved 100% by His grace, not my performance, and the Holy Spirit will keep me secure until Jesus returns to fix the world."

Version 3: Spirit-Filled Leaning (Gentle) "I believe God is our loving Father who created us for relationship. When sin broke the world, Jesus stepped in, defeated death on the cross, and rose again to set us free. Today, the Holy Spirit actually lives inside of me, giving me the power to overcome sin, experience God's presence, and share His love with others while we wait for Jesus to return and heal the world completely."

Appendix C: Glossary (Teen-Friendly Theological Terms)

(*You don't have to go to seminary to know what these words mean. Use this as your personal cheat sheet when reading the Bible or listening to a sermon!*)

Cost of Discipleship: The things you willingly give up, like comfort, popularity, or control over your own life, in order to follow Jesus.

- *Precision Note:* Popularized by theologian Dietrich Bonhoeffer, contrasting "costly grace" against "cheap grace."

Discernment: The ability to judge well between multiple options, especially when choosing between "good" and "best" rather than just "right" and "wrong."

- *Precision Note:* A spiritual sensitivity cultivated by the Holy Spirit and deep familiarity with Scripture.

The Fall: The moment human beings rebelled against God, fracturing everything. It is the reason the world is infected with disease, cruelty, natural disasters, and death.

- *Precision Note:* Rooted in Genesis 3, referring to the introduction of systemic physical and spiritual corruption into the human experience.

Final Judgment: The moment at the end of history when Jesus will perfectly and fairly evaluate every human life and permanently eliminate evil.

- *Precision Note:* A cosmic event that publically vindicates God's righteousness.

Hell: Eternal separation from the presence, goodness, and grace of God.

- *Precision Note:* A state of active judgment against unrepentant rebellion, where those who rejected God are given exactly what they demanded: existence without Him.

Holiness: Being set apart and looking distinctly different from the world around you because you are reflecting the character of Jesus.

- *Precision Note:* Derived from the Hebrew root word qadosh, meaning to be separated, cut off, or dedicated to a sacred purpose.

Idolatry: Treating a good thing (like your friendships, your grades, or your reputation) as an ultimate thing that you can't live without.

- *Precision Note:* The primary sin addressed throughout Scripture; replacing the Creator with creation as the source of identity and security.

The Incarnation: The historic event where the eternal Son of God became a human being in Jesus Christ.

- *Precision Note:* The union of divine and human natures in the single person of Christ.

The Intermediate State: The temporary period of time between a person's physical death and the future day when Jesus returns to resurrect our bodies.

- *Precision Note:* During this time, the souls of believers are fully conscious and in the immediate presence of Christ.

Justification: God's legal declaration that you are completely forgiven and righteous, not because you earned it, but because Jesus gave you His perfect record.

- *Precision Note:* A one-time, forensic act of God received by faith alone.

Lament: A passionate, unfiltered expression of grief, anger, or sorrow directed toward God.

- *Precision Note:* A major biblical genre comprising roughly a third of the Psalms.

Mortality: The state of being subject to death; the reality that our physical bodies will eventually fail and die.

- *Precision Note:* Physical death was introduced as a direct consequence of the Fall (Genesis 3), severing the body from the soul.

New Heavens and New Earth: The final, eternal state of the universe where God's realm and the human realm are permanently fused together in physical perfection.

- *Precision Note:* Described in Revelation 21, this represents the culmination of God's redemptive plan.

Restoration: The process of taking something broken and returning it to its original, perfect design.

- *Precision Note:* The Greek word *palingenesia*, meaning "rebirth" or "renewal" of the cosmos.

Revealed Will: The clear commands and instructions God has already given us in the Bible (e.g., love your enemies, do not steal).

- *Precision Note:* Distinguished from God's "hidden will" or "sovereign will," which includes the secret details of the future.

Sanctification: The slow, lifelong process of becoming more like Jesus and leaving your old sinful habits behind.

- *Precision Note:* A progressive, cooperative work of the Holy Spirit and the believer.

Shalom: The Hebrew concept of universal flourishing, wholeness, and absolute peace where nothing is missing and nothing is broken.

- *Precision Note:* The vibrant, joyous harmony of humans, nature, and God.

Trinity: The truth that there is only one God, who eternally exists as three distinct persons: God the Father, God the Son, and God the Holy Spirit.

- *Precision Note:* The central mystery of the Christian faith; God is one in essence, three in person.

Wisdom: The practical skill of living life well in God's world; knowing what is right, what is good, and how to apply it to real-life situations.

Appendix D: Leader/Parent Guide

How to help your teens build their theology without hijacking the process.

The 8-Week Small Group Plan

If you are leading a youth group, a Sunday school class, or doing this with your own teenager at home, here is an 8-week pacing guide. (Have the teens read the assigned chapters *before* you meet).

- **Week 1: The Foundation.** Discuss Chapter 0.1, 0.2, and Part 1 (The Bible). *Goal: Establish a safe environment for hard questions.*
- **Week 2: Who is God?** Discuss Part 2 (God). *Goal: Dismantle small views of God and discuss the Trinity without getting weird.*
- **Week 3: The Problem.** Discuss Part 3 (People & Sin). *Goal: Help teens understand that sin is more than just breaking rules; it's a broken relationship.*
- **Week 4: The Hero.** Discuss Part 4 (Jesus). *Goal: Focus heavily on the reality of the resurrection.*
- **Week 5: The Gift.** Discuss Part 5 (Salvation) & Part 6 (Holy Spirit). *Goal: Ensure every teen understands that grace cannot be earned.*
- **Week 6: The Family.** Discuss Part 7 (The Church). *Goal: Talk honestly about church hurt and why the local church still matters.*
- **Week 7: The Real World.** Discuss Part 8 (The Christian Life). *Goal: Share your own stories of suffering, doubting, and needing God's wisdom.*
- **Week 8: The Endgame.** Discuss Part 9 (Last Things) & Part 10 (Capstone). *Goal: Have a "Statement of Faith" party. Have teens read their 30-Second scripts out loud.*

3 Rules for Leading Without Hijacking

1. **Never answer your own question immediately.** Teenagers need time to process. Ask a question, and then endure the awkward silence. Count to ten in your head before speaking again. Someone *will* talk.

2. **Don't polish their bricks.** When a teen shares their "Belief Builder" brick, do not correct their grammar or try to make it sound "more theological." If it is orthodox, affirm it. If they own the language, they will own the belief.

3. **Be honest about your own doubts.** The most powerful thing a youth leader can say is, "I've struggled with that exact same question, and it was terrifying. Here is how God carried me through it", or even, "I still wrestle with that sometimes, but here is why I still choose to trust Jesus."

How to Handle the "Hard Questions"

When a teenager asks a question you don't know the answer to (e.g., *What about the dinosaurs? Why did God allow my grandpa to die? How does predestination work?*), follow this playbook:

- **Validate the question:** "That is a brilliant question. I'm so glad you asked that."

- **Confess your limits:** "To be completely honest, I don't know the exact answer to that right now."

- **Commit to the journey:** "But I want to find out. Let's look into this together this week, and we will talk about what we find next Wednesday."

- **Pivot to the anchor:** "Even when we don't understand the mysteries of how God works, what do we know for sure based on the resurrection?"

www.ingramcontent.com/pod-product-compliance
Ingram Content Group UK Ltd.
Pitfield, Milton Keynes, MK11 3LW, UK
UKHW051138260726
13967UKWH00010B/3119

9 781963 142327